ERA: May a State Change Its Vote?

Samuel S. Freedman   &   Pamela J. Naughton

MAY A STATE CHANGE ITS VOTE?

Wayne State University Press   *Detroit*

Library of Congress Cataloging in Publication Data

Freedman, Samuel S   1927–

    ERA, may a state change its vote?

    (Waynebook ; 46)

    Includes bibliographical references and index.

    1. Sex discrimination against women—Law and legislation—United States. 2. United States—Constitutional law—Amendments. I. Naughton, Pamela J., 1954– joint author. I. Title.

KF4758.F73   342',73'087   78–10821

ISBN 0–8143–1623–9

ISBN 0–8143–1624–7 pbk.

Waynebook 46

For Judi, Martha, and Harry Freedman—for so many reasons—with love
and
For Millie Mrja, who personifies courage, dignity, enthusiasm,
and unselfish love

Contents

Appendices

Chapter 1

ERA in Perspective:
The Background of Rescission

After some fifty years of preparation, the proposed "equal rights amendment" (ERA) has made a substantial impact on American public life. It first swept through the nation like a twister, easily eliminating obstacles in its path. Politician and legislative body alike fell, not to the compelling nature of its argument but to fear of the unknown: the potential political backlash of opposing the perceived desires of at least half of the voters—the country's women. Thus is history made.

But action often produces reaction. The prevailing winds were cooled by a countervailing force of considerable velocity. With the emergence of a well-financed, highly organized opposition, women pleased by the benefits of what they had viewed as newly found freedoms were dismayed by arguments setting forth a parade of horrible consequences which, they were told, would accompany the amendment. Although it was late in the day, the issue was joined, experts were assembled for battle, and the first real debate began.

With the approach of the March 1979 deadline set by Congress, the backers of ERA, once certain it would become the twenty-seventh amendment to the Constitution, found its force diminished and their progress slowed. Still, the idea did not die easily, nor was its movement totally checked. It was at this point in history that the seldom used extraconstitutional doctrine of *rescission* was revived. The Nebraska, Tennessee, and Idaho legislatures had all voted to rescind their previous ratifications. With only three more states needed to ratify, opponents of the amendment attempted to breathe new life into a doctrine nowhere mentioned in the Constitution itself. The final chapter on rescission has not yet been written.

American federal history has produced its semidoctrines, grounded partly in historical precedent and partly in logic, but fueled mainly by expedient policy-oriented desires. Some have seen only partial, temporary success, but almost all have exploded upon the American scene and somehow left it changed. The list is short but significant. *Nullification* (by states of federal law) shook the very foundations of the early 1800s. Its shock waves were felt for years and led to unparalleled brutality on the battlefields of the Civil War. Years later, a more adult United States faced the battles fought over *executive privilege*—from the internments and business take-overs of the Roosevelt-Truman 1940s, to the foreign interventionism of the Kennedy-Johnson 1960s, to the trauma of the Nixon 1970s. Few nations could have survived this explosive era without upheaval. That we did so with relative calm and a minimum of interference in the constitutional prescription is a tribute not just to the American people, but to the genius of the document under which we live and to the small handful of men whose brilliance created it. We have learned that the Constitution works.

It is doubtful that the idea of rescission will cause upheavals comparable to those created by these other issues. It rests, nevertheless, in that same semidoctrinal constitutional never-never land and requires resolution. Until it is put to rest one way or the other, the underlying controversy, the fight over equal rights for women, will not be clearly seen. Both sides in the conflict have set up enough smokescreens to cloud most of the relevant issues. We are willing to predict that ERA can find three more state legislatures to support it, and the stage will be set for the next great American constitutional debate: the validity of the doctrine of the rescission of a constitutional amendment.

The provisions of ERA are simply stated in their entirety.

Section One. Equality of rights under the law shall not be denied or abridged by the United States or by any state on account of sex.

Section Two. The Congress shall have the power to enforce by appropriate legislation the provisions of this article.

Section Three. This amendment shall take effect two years after the date of ratification.

On 22 March 1972, the United States Senate overwhelmingly completed action on House Joint Resolution 208, which submitted the proposed ERA to the states after one of the longest gestation periods in American constitutional history. Adoption now lacks only three states of the required thirty-eight ratifications due by 22 March 1979. But of the thirty-five assenters, four states have adopted resolutions attempting to rescind their ratifications: Nebraska on 15 March 1973 (thirty-one to seventeen), Tennessee on 23 April 1974 (by one vote in the senate and six in the house) and, more recently, Idaho, on 8 February 1977. Idaho legislators, under considerable pressure from a highly successful lobbying effort by the Mormon church, took the unusual step of changing the rule requiring a two-thirds vote to one requiring a simple majority. A one-vote victory in the state senate attested to the wisdom of their action and their political acumen in counting votes. On 16 March 1978, the Kentucky senate approved and sent to the governor House Joint Resolution 20, which dealt with state pensions but also included an amendment from the floor rescinding Kentucky's ratification of ERA. Lieutenant Governor Thelma Stovall, acting in the governor's absence, vetoed the resolution. She claimed that it violated the state constitution, which prohibits the General Assembly from passing any law dealing with more than one subject, and that it also violated a senate rule which prohibits the introduction of new bills within the last ten days of the legislative session. Both the resolution and the veto message were sent by the secretary of state of Kentucky to the federal General Services Administration.

Recently ratified by Indiana, ERA met legislative defeat at the hands of fifteen other states: Missouri, Illinois, Nevada, North Carolina, Oklahoma, Virginia, Georgia, Louisiana, Arkansas, Arizona, Alabama, Mississippi, South Carolina, Utah, and Florida. Faced for the most part with the need to continue its progress in southern and western states, where antagonistic pressure groups have tended to produce less than sympathetic legislatures, those favoring the amendment are finding that the road ahead, while not blocked, is surely rocky. Those familiar with both Congress and the state capitols know how exquisitely sensitive legislators are to political pressure.

Luckily for ERA supporters, that rocky road is now a short one. It may not be easy to block ratification by three sister states. The validity of the three rescission attempts will then be forced into the critical spotlight of national examination, and it is highly likely that incorporation of the amendment into the Constitution will depend squarely on the outcome of that scrutiny. Once again a massive constitutional crisis is in prospect, this time fired by a press keenly aware of its publicity value, women's organizations determined to see their child survive, a president in Washington deeply committed to adoption of that child, and men and women on and off college campuses who equate ERA's success with the support of basic freedoms. The organizational prowess of their opponents, armed by constitutional experts, self-proclaimed and otherwise, assures that the debate will be hard, loud, lengthy, and most of all, decisive. Resort to the courts is a surety. What the courts will do is less than sure. They could do nothing, returning the ball to Congress where it all began.

Those actively working on the state level are keenly aware that legal opinions are sometimes overcome by legislative decision making. Nebraska,

Tennessee, and Idaho solicited opinions from their attorneys general prior to taking action on rescission, all of whom concurred in believing that those rescission attempts would ultimately be adjudged invalid. Did the rescinding lawmakers simply disagree? Were they registering a symbolic disapproval? Did they yield to lobbying pressures and what they saw to be political expediency, thereby pacifying opponents while remaining confident that their vote would bear no legal force? The questions are intriguing in what they suggest about legislative behavior.

The arguments of those who believe that rescissions are valid—rescissionists—take several tacks. Charles Black of the Yale Law School refers to the "absurdity" of finality in ratification, relying with former Senator Sam Ervin of North Carolina on common sense and fairness (see Appendix D). The colorful Mr. Ervin, the Senate's longtime constitutional expert, asserts that what is "sauce for the constitutional goose" is "sauce for the constitutional gander." Thus, if a state can reject and later ratify, fairness dictates its ability to ratify and later reject. But there is little legal precedent for common sense. The argument is also made that rescission as a subsequent action reflects a change in public opinion and is therefore valid. Logically extended, this becomes a "whoever has the final say can win" argument.

The Ervin thesis further asserts that because no Supreme Court decision explicitly sets forth the finality of ratification, any state may rescind up to the time three-fourths of them have assented and thereby formed the compact necessary for constitutional amendment. There is a "universal rule", he argues, "that a state legislative body cannot bind itself or any future legislative body permanently by any action which it may take in respect to any matter." The argument is not without documentation, but it leads to a serious question. Is a state legislature acting as a state legislative body when ratifying a constitutional amendment, or is it performing a federal function, federally prescribed? Is there any historical or legal precedent for Ervin's assertion?

Finally, goes the argument, if a state believes it has acted too hastily, it should be allowed to revise its action after more sober consideration. After all, amendments are too important to be left to temporary whim. There is just a hint here of legislative reaction to the will of the public. This raises still another question of more than passing interest. Just how responsive are legislatures to public opinion? The importance of the answer clearly goes far beyond the passage of ERA or any individual amendment.

Chapter 2

The Ratification Process

Article V of the Constitution of the United States explicitly prescribes the exclusive means to effect an amendment.

The Congress, whenever two-thirds of both houses shall deem it necessary, shall propose amendments to this Constitution, or, on the application of the legislatures of two-thirds of the several states, shall call a convention for proposing amendments, which, in either case, shall be valid to all intents and purposes, as part of this Constitution, when ratified by the legislatures of three-fourths of the several states, or by conventions in three-fourths thereof, as the one or the other mode of ratification may be proposed by the Congress; provided that no amendment which may be made prior to the year one thousand eight hundred and eight shall in any manner affect the first and fourth clauses in the ninth section of the first article; and that no state, without its consent, shall be deprived of its equal suffrage in the Senate.

There exist then, side by side, two methods of proposing amendments: 1) by joint resolution, approved by two-thirds of both houses of Congress; and 2) by convention, called on the application of two-thirds of the state legislatures. While this second option has never been exercised, several of the 304 amendments proposed under it nearly garnered enough state approvals to make it operational. A reapportionment amendment attracted applications for a convention from thirty-three states between 1957 and 1969; direct senatorial elections totaled thirty-one applications from 1893 to 1911; and enough male-dominated legislatures agreed with an apparent feminine view that one wife is enough so that even the prohibition of polygamy found support from twenty-seven states between 1906 and 1916.

There are also only two methods prescribed for ratification: either approval of three-fourths of the legislatures or approval of three-fourths of state conventions called exclusively for the purpose of ratification. The latter has been used only in the case of the Twenty-First Amendment, when it was deemed appropriate to submit the question of repealing the Eighteenth Amendment directly to the people. Presently there are no federal statutes or regulations setting forth procedures for the convention method of ratification.

Courts have universally construed Article V narrowly, agreeing that states cannot use alternative forms of ratification, such as referenda. When the Justices of the Maine Supreme Court *(In Re Opinion of the Justices)** reviewed a Maine constitutional provision providing for a referendum to validate a ratification, they accepted without argument, although begging the question somewhat, the premise that since a state lacks the power to rescind a ratification it cannot be done by referendum. Legislative inability to rescind ratification by a prior legislature, said the court, indicates "that much less could such ratification be rescinded by the subsequent vote of the people," especially since the "people have unreservedly surrendered all authority over that subject matter." A 1974 Montana decision *(Hatch v. Murray)* subsequently defeated a challenge that ERA was not put to the people, while a North Dakota case *(Askew v. Meir)* held in 1975 that such a referendum could be used as a nonbinding straw vote. It is interesting that Idaho, a rescinding state, has a new provision requiring a purely advisory referendum. The idea presumably emerged from the rescissionists' thesis that changes in public opinion should be mirrored by appropriate legislative action.

Any broad constructionist view of Article V must ultimately come to grips with the fact that there is no provision for, nor mention made of, rescission. The Constitution, the argument goes, is necessarily vague to gain the flexibility needed to cope with changing times and orders. This position, unhappily, faces a special problem with Article V because the framers included three very specific exceptions in the article: the prohibition, until 1808, of passage of antislavery or tax amendments and of any amendment affecting equal suffrage in the Senate. This is, in fact, one of the most specific parts of the mother document. It is not unreasonable to argue, as lawyers do every day, that this kind of specificity indicates clear limitations. Thus, if rescission was intended to be viable, it too would have been spelled out in Article V.

The question of the framers' intent is fascinating, although its probative value and documentation in the legal arena are questionable. Courts driving hard toward a judicial opinion have often noted that the meaning of legislation is to be found not in what was intended but what was actually said. In that case, we must inescapably conclude that rescission simply doesn't exist. Yet no one should be surprised that other jurists finding statements of intent fully supportive of their position have quoted them

*See Appendices E and F for full citations to legal cases and other sources.

freely in judicial decisions. Is there any such support for the doctrine of rescission?

James Madison's notes on the debates during the Constitutional Convention of 1787 indicate its suspicions of allowing Congress to propose amendments; rather, it preferred the convention method as the sole mechanism of proposal. Later Alexander Hamilton, not long emigrated from the Caribbean islands of Nevis and Saint Croix, spoke eloquently of facilitating the amendment process through congressional sensitivity to the people who were, after all, the sole masters to be served. Madison records that, looking back, Hamilton reflected that it "was much to have been desired that an easier mode for introducing amendments had been provided by the Articles of Confederation" (p. 609) (unanimous ratification was required). The authorization for congressional proposal was added without further debate. Facilitation of the amendment process was clearly the final intent. Would the impeding of adoption by rescission actually fall contrary to that intent? Or can one read into rescission a means of better serving the people of a state by providing a governmental response for a public change of heart?

The convention debate centered on the proposing of amendments. Does this indicate that the delegates held similar views on the question of ratifications? Probably. Their unequivocal description in Article V makes it difficult to argue that the subject was overlooked. Rather, proposal was felt to be the real problem. But clearly the majority appeared to believe that Congress should have ultimate control of the amending process. Colonel George Mason of Virginia, an opponent of the plan speaking for the minority, found it dangerous since "the proposing of amendments is in both the modes to depend, in the first immediately, in the second, ultimately, on Congress." No proper amendments, he opined, "would ever be obtained by the people, if the Government should become oppressive"(p. 69).

Since neither *The Federalist* nor any state constitutional conventions recorded any debates specifically on the issue of rescission, we are inevitably left with Article V itself as the best indicator of intent. Its message, clear and unmistakable, is that adoption of an amendment automatically follows ratification by the requisite number of states. The United States Supreme Court (in a case hotly debated today by opponents of ERA) adopted this view in the case of *Coleman* v. *Miller* (1939), holding:

> We find no basis in either constitution or statute for such judicial action. Article V, speaking solely of ratification, contains no provision as to rejection. Nor has the Congress enacted a statute relating to rejection.

The last sentence may be as important as the first. The court clearly indicated its belief that Congress had the right to enact legislation relative to the validity of rescissions if it wished.

Only one federal statute has been enacted under the aegis of Article V (excepting the reorganization plan which removed the function of proclaiming amendments from the office of the secretary of state and gave it to the Administrator of General Services). Title 1, United States Code, Section 106b (31 October 1951) states:

> Whenever official notice is received at the General Services Administration, that any amendment proposed to the Constitution of the United States has been adopted, according to the provisions of the Constitution, the Administrator of General Services shall forthwith cause the amendment to be published, with his certificate, specifying the States by which the same may have been adopted, and that the same has become valid, to all intents and purposes, as a part of the Constitution of the United States.

The critical words for purposes of rescission appear to be ''according to the provisions of the Constitution.'' It can be argued that Congress overlooked the question of rejection by states, but the statute's plain instruction is to follow the literal wording of the Constitution, which simply leaves no room for the legality of any such subsequent rejections. No other federal statutes exist.

Has Congress ever attempted to clarify the subject of rescission? The answer, surprisingly, is yes. In 1870 a bill recognizing the validity of rescission passed the House, only to die in the Senate Committee on the Judiciary. Another, debated in 1924, failed to reach a vote in either house. Although former Senator Ervin maintains that states already have the right to rescind prior ratifications, in 1967, 1969, 1971, and 1973 he introduced bills (all referred to his own Judiciary Subcommittee on Separation of Powers rather than the Subcommittee on Constitutional Amendments) which made provision for this situation. The latter two were approved and sent to the Senate floor, with one passing in 1971, eighty-four to nothing. None has escaped the House Judiciary Committee.

Providing for convention ratifying mechanisms, the Ervin measures also included (Sec. 13) the right of a state to rescind a prior ratification if the requisite three-fourths of the states had not yet acted affirmatively, and another provision which stated, not inconsistently:

> Questions concerning state ratification or rejection of amendments proposed to the Constitution of the United States, shall be determined solely by the Congress of the United States, and its decisions shall be binding on all others, including State and Federal Courts.

It is possible that Senator Ervin was simply trying to set forth in statute what he considered in any event to be the law. However, in light of his contention that the issue is justiciable since the entrance of the Supreme Court into the "political question" arena in *Baker* v. *Carr* (on reapportionment) and the Adam Clayton Powell case, it is also possible that he has changed his mind since his congressional days. His subcommittee report argued: "It is the opinion of the committee that Congress unquestionably has the authority to legislate about the process of amendment by convention, and to settle every point not actually settled by Article V of the Constitution itself. This is implicit in Article V" (See Appendix C). The report seems to imply that the question of rescission is not only politically excluded from the courtroom, but so politically unacceptable as a legal issue that recognition of its validity demands a special congressional act. Unless the subcommittee felt the congressional process was not exclusive, which the words of its report seem to rebut, Ervin's contention that rescission and its ability to be heard by the courts are a matter of reason and pure common sense probably indicates that he has undergone a change in view since he dropped the reins of his Senate subcommittee.

This analysis is supported by a series of articles on the Ervin bill in the March 1968 issue of the *Michigan Law Review*. One of the contributing writers was Senator Ervin. The articles discussed the gathering of petitions from sufficient states to call a constitutional convention for drafting an amendment to overturn the reapportionment case of *Reynolds* v. *Sims*. By 1967 only two petitions were needed for the convention, and the Ervin bill, filed 17 August 1967, attempted, among other things, to set procedures for this convention.

Some writers questioned Congress's authority to dictate procedures to the convention when the convention method itself was established to circumvent Congress. In justifying his approach favoring congressional determination, the senator recognized "the weight of such decisions as *Coleman* v. *Miller*, to the effect that questions arising in the amending process are nonjusticiable political questions exclusively in the congressional domain" (p. 880). Ervin appears to conclude: "The Supreme Court has held that questions concerning the rescission of prior ratifications or rejections of amendments proposed by the Congress are determinable solely by Congress" (p. 889). The line of "political" reapportionment cases had already come, but in fairness, one must remember both that the decision in the Adam Clayton Powell case had yet to be handed down and that the senator offered a caveat in the *Michigan Law Review,* saying that he was "not committed to the provisions of the bill as then drafted," but was convinced of the need for action (p. 879).

Not all constitutional experts considered opposed to ERA agree with Senator Ervin's recent exposition of the rescission question. Paul Freund of Harvard Law School, in a letter to the late Senator Philip Hart during the subcommittee hearings on the Ervin bill, noted the historical precedent of the Fourteenth Amendment and concluded: "[The refusal to honor rescissions] seemed to me not illogical since a rejection has no formal constitutional status while a ratification does." Thomas I. Emerson, professor emeritus of the Yale Law School, while firmly in the pro-ERA ranks, agrees on the subject of rescission. In testimony before the Connecticut legislature's Committee on Government Administration and Policy on 16 March 1977, he analogized the amendment process to contract law: "If a salesman for the Encyclopedia Britannica comes to your door you may turn him down three times; but if you accept the fourth time you are bound by that action and you cannot rescind."

Courts have often found the offer-and-acceptance of contract law with which Emerson earmarked the amending process a useful analogy. A state, by entering into a compact with other states to adopt an amendment, has bound itself and caused other states to rely on that action. "Proposal and ratification," said the Supreme Court (*Dillon* v. *Gloss*) in 1920, "are not treated as separate acts but as succeeding steps in a single endeavor." The argument has been made that a state cannot rescind without affecting other states, both those in privity with it and those which did not act, relying on its ratification. This argument also points to the possible detrimental reliance of citizens of a ratifying state, who, believing the issue settled, turn their political attentions elsewhere, thereby leaving themselves vulnerable to unforeseen lobbying efforts by rescissionists at a late hour. The argument is not without a certain compelling charm. But the Emerson thesis falls somewhat short. After all, contract law and the amending process are not the same thing. There is a good deal beyond offer-and-acceptance which simply doesn't apply: mutuality, sufficiency of consideration, mitigation, and the whole subject of damages. To some extent, Emerson's argument resembles an attempt to compare apples and oranges. The best one can say is that they both bear fruit.

There is yet another argument put forth in behalf of rescission, which is that states should be allowed to change their ratification upon a realization that their original action was too hastily taken. This presumably assumes that public opinion has shifted on the issue. The "hastiness" argument cuts both ways. Even disregarding the obvious fact that ERA had been before the Congress for some fifty years, allowing abundant time for public consideration, Nebraska's rescission could hardly be called less hasty than its ratification, both of which occurred within one year. There is another consideration. If a legislator knows his ratification vote can always be rescinded, would he be more likely to succumb to the immediacy of lobbying pressures, thus substituting political expediency for rational deliberation? Doesn't the stamping of ratification with finality impose the kind of deliberate, rational decision making upon legislators that an issue as weighty as a constitutional amendment deserves?

If early ratification can be dangerous because it is undertaken too hastily, how does early rescission differ? Speaking of New York's attempted rescission of the Fifteenth Amendment (black suffrage), Senator Roscoe Conkling told his fellow senators: "I avow my regret that a record of action so hasty, so ill-advised and so nugatory should come here at all, and my greater regret that it should come from the State capitol of New York."

Only in modern times, with the advent of the Eighteenth Amendment, has Congress attached a time limit to the ratification of amendments. If in the future it does not, would the validation of rescission have any adverse effects? When, in effect, must a state stop changing its mind? In the absence of a directive, who decides when the scrambling ceases? Presumably such questions led to a congressionally imposed time limitation, an action clearly upheld in *Dillon* v. *Gloss*.

Legislative reaction to the public will is itself fascinating. Do legislatures know what the public wants? Will they in fact accede to its wishes? A look at the situation in Connecticut should be enough to confuse anyone. Connecticut's constitution requires the legislature's adoption of state constitutional amendments to be ratified by a binding, nonrescindable referendum. Faced with such an amendment, the voters overwhelmingly defeated a proposal to give eighteen-year-olds the right to vote. Yet less than one year later, Connecticut's legislature was one of the first to ratify the same question when it appeared as an amendment to the U.S. Constitution. Was the public annoyed by this obvious rejection of their will? Hardly. It was apathetic. The assumption that state legislatures accurately reflect public opinion may well be suspect. Even if they do, is there any reason to believe that Congress does so less? If rescission is deemed a political question for Congress, and the mood of the country has swung away from ratification of ERA since the time of proposal, should Congress be the proper body to answer the requests for withdrawal? It too is a political organ, answerable to the electorate. Could Congress also withdraw the proposal prior to ratification by three-fourths of the states?

Finally, if the mood of the country has changed so radically, what about the recourse to repeal of an amendment in the manner used against Prohibition? This solution may be shocking to constitutional purists, but it may be a better way of infusing cautious deliberation into the amendment process while still responding to the public will. The framers did not mean constitutional amendments to be taken lightly. Legislators were more properly meant to follow the old adage: "Be slow in making up your mind and even slower in changing it."

Critical to this discussion is the specific role played by the state legislatures in ratifying amendments. This much is clear: ratification is a *federal function* under which legislatures, acting as parts of the federal union, *act according to federal prescription.* In a sense, the function imposed upon them by the Constitution puts a state legislature into the position of a federally mandated convention, rather than of a self-governing entity. A legislature says yea or nay to a proposed constitutional addition. It may not amend it or change it in any way. It is, then, acting as an agent of the federal government in the process of changing the basic document under which the union as a whole, not the state alone, exists. This is not a legislative function governed by state rules for the making of state law.

Federal Supreme Court acceptance of this principle came in 1922 in the now famous case of *Leser* v. *Garnett*, which held that state ratification attempts were restricted by federal law. West Virginia's ratification of the Nineteenth Amendment (enfranchisement of women) was challenged because its prior rejection by the state senate in the same session violated a rule of that senate (common to most legislatures) prohibiting the consideration of any issue more than once during a given session. Finding that ratification did not constitute an act of legislation and was therefore not subject to state constraints, the high court held: "[T]he function of a state legislature in ratifying . . . like the function of Congress in proposing the amendment is a federal function derived from the Federal Constitution; and it transcends any limitations sought to be imposed by the people of a State."

The Kentucky Supreme Court reiterated this view in 1937 in *Wise* v. *Chandler.* Deciding upon the finality of a vote upon an amendment, it spoke of the federal function of a legislature acting as a ratifying convention, and declared: "[W]hen a Legislature, sitting, not as a lawmaking body, but as such an assembly, has acted upon a proposal for an amendment, it likewise has exhausted its power in this connection." The court's assertion that state legislatures are functioning as ratifying conventions assumes the finality of ratification, since conventions, in parliamentry law, upon voting to ratify adjourn sine die in the absence of authority in Article V allowing them to reconsider.

There is, of course, an offshoot of this doctrine. Detractors of ERA, anxious for rescission to succeed, have grasped the doctrine of contemporaneity to justify legislative action. Simply stated, this means that adoption or rejection of an amendment should follow the latest wishes of the people. After all, legislatures every day reverse themselves with changes in the public opinion polls. (Not only the Supreme Court follows the election returns, Mr. Dooley.) But as early as 1920, the Supreme Court in *Hawke* v. *Smith* found a postratification referendum on the Eighteenth Amendment invalid, with the comment: "[R]atification by a State . . . is not an act of legislation within the proper sense of the word. It is but the expression of the assent of the State to a proposed amendment." Thus legislative revisionism is limited to the act of lawmaking and prohibited during the amendment process. This casts grave doubt on the "common sense" argument that rejection after ratification is an expression of a change in public opinion and little different from ratification after rejection. Ratification and legislation are simply not the same thing. They are subject to different procedures.

There are several other areas in the ratification conflict that deserve mention. All agree that once three-fourths of the states have ratified an amendment, a compact exists and rescission is no longer possible. This clearly is in conflict with theories of contemporaneity which would allow a state to exhibit a change of heart whenever it chooses. But even opponents of ERA concede a period of finality. And administrative confusion alone demands an end to the process at some point. Otherwise the problems ensuing from a rash of ratifications and rescissions at the last minute before the deadline for ratification would be unbearable. In fact, a strong argument for disallowing rescission has been made on the basis of just such confusion in the administering of the law.

It is also settled that an amendment is adopted at that point in time when the Administrator of General Services receives notice of the requisite number of ratifications. It does not depend upon his proclamation, a presidential proclamation, or a joint resolution of Congress, although all three have been used in the past with no general pattern or rationale. In the case of *U.S. ex rel. Widenmann* v. *Colby* in 1921, the United States Supreme Court, faced with an attempt to prevent the secretary of state from issuing a proclamation of adoption of the Eighteenth Amendment on the grounds of improper ratification and invalid notice to the secretary, struck down the claim by limiting the effectiveness of the proclamation. "It is the approval of the requisite number of states, not the proclamation that gives vitality to the amendment and makes it a part of the supreme law of the land."

The Vermont Supreme Court, in the later case of *Chase* v. *Billings* (1934), found a challenge to ratifying procedures moot once the secretary of state received notice of ratification.

> [W]hen he received like notice from the requisite number of states, the ratification of the proposed amendment was consummated, and became, to all intents and purposes, part of the Federal Constitution. . . . The Secretary's proclamation certifying the states that had ratified the proposed amendment was official notice to the world of what had happened, and, as we have seen, is conclusive upon the courts.

Finally, no one seriously questions that the ultimate determination of the validity of legislative treatment of a proposed amendment cannot be left to the Administrator of General Services. His is a purely ministerial function; he has no authority to investigate or rule upon a state's action. The *Widenmann* v. *Colby* case declared: "As soon as he had received the notices from 36 of the states that the amendment had been adopted, he was obliged, under the statute, to put forth his proclamation." According to Article V and statute, therefore, the Administrator's power is limited to recording ratifications; and upon duly counting the requisite number of such notices, it is incumbent upon him to issue a proclamation of adoption. Unless the courts reverse this stance, it would appear that when three more states ratify ERA, the Administrator must proclaim it adopted. Nowhere is he given power to count or subtract rejections or rescissions.

Chapter 3

Congressional Precedent

At only one point in the history of the United States could the recognition of states rescinding their ratification have prevented the adoption of an amendment. The episode involved the Fourteenth Amendment, which has been directly responsible for more judicial interpretation of constitutional, criminal, and administrative law than any other. Cases touched by its requirements of due process and equal protection run literally into the millions.

The historical background is highly significant. Assent by twenty-eight of the thirty-seven states then in the Union was required for adoption. In post-Civil War America, after Georgia, North Carolina, and South Carolina rejected the amendment in December 1866, renewal of congressional representation for those Confederate states was made dependent upon their ratification of the Fourteenth Amendment. This harsh condition led them one by one to its adoption: North Carolina on 4 July 1868; South Carolina and Louisiana on 9 July 1868; Alabama on 13 July 1868; and Georgia on 21 July 1868. Meanwhile, New Jersey's 11 September 1866 ratification was "withdrawn" (rescinded) in April 1868, and Ohio, which ratified on 11 January 1867, rescinded on 15 January 1868.

Upon receipt of notice of the 9 July ratifications of Louisiana and South Carolina, the twenty-seventh and twenty-eighth ratifying states, Secretary William H. Seward prepared a proclamation declaring the Fourteenth Amendment adopted, although the adoption was contingent upon ignoring the withdrawals of New Jersey and Ohio. (By the time it was issued on 20 July, Alabama's ratification constituted a total of twenty-nine states.) Seward noted in the preamble of his proclamation: "[I]t is deemed a matter of doubt and uncertainty whether such resolutions are not irregular, invalid, and therefore ineffectual for withdrawing the consent of the said two States, or either of them, to the aforesaid amendment." He then made the proclamation conditional:

[I]f the resolutions of the legislatures of Ohio and New Jersey ratifying the aforesaid amendment are to be deemed as remaining of full force and effect, notwithstanding the subsequent resolutions of the legislatures of those States, which purport to withdraw the consent of said States from such ratification, then the aforesaid amendment has been ratified in the manner hereinbefore mentioned, and so has become valid, to all intents and purposes, as a part of the Constitution of the United States.

This proclamation was sent to Congress by Seward to resolve the issue, and considered there the next day, 21 July 1868. The Senate approved all twenty-nine states without debate. The record fails to show any mention of the attempted New Jersey or Ohio rescissions, nor does it indicate senatorial awareness of Georgia's approval that very day. The Senate sent it on to the House of Representatives as a concurrent resolution, where it was considered later that day. However, examination of the list which was read in the House reveals that a routine procedure was, in fact, highly irregular. The list did not include South Carolina or Alabama. One can only conclude that the resolution approved by the House was not the same one approved by the Senate. Since only twenty-seven states appeared on the House resolution, it appears that that body ignored the dictates of the Constitution by approving a resolution before it which on its face was patently illegal, lacking a showing of ratification by the necessary three-fourths of the states.

What does this mean? No other commentators have remarked on this discrepancy, so there has been no reaction to it. A simple explanation could be that there is a misprint or error in transcription, but this does not escape the important fact that the House considered the rescissions of New Jersey and Ohio and voted to ignore them. The decision seems to have been arrived at consciously. Rescission opponents could, of course, argue that this error destroys the action as a precedent against rescission. It seems unlikely that they will, however, because the corollary to the success of their argument would be nullification of the Fourteenth Amendment, and a massive body of law has been built up around it.

Unlike the Senate, the House, realizing the gravity of the rescission question, first discussed sending the resolution to the Reconstruction or Judiciary Committee. The Speaker of the House, however, received a telegram from Georgia's governor-elect informing him of its instant ratification of the Fourteenth Amendment, which caused the referral idea to be abandoned without vote in favor of discussing the inclusion of Georgia in the list of states. Had the resolution read correctly, Georgia would have been the thirtieth state, therefore eliminating the need to consider the two rescissions. Realizing this, Congressman James Brooks of New York objected to reading the telegram into the record "unless we have read the withdrawal by Ohio and New Jersey of their assent to that amendment.'' While his remark was ignored and the telegram read, the motion to insert Georgia into the resolution failed because of serious doubts about its official nature. Parliamentary ingenuity then took over. A motion to separate the preamble containing the list from the resolution passed and the resolution itself was then passed. After approval of the resolution, the House approved the preamble without further debate.

The resolution itself listed no states, but merely concurred with the Senate resolution. Both were sent to the secretary of state, who issued the adoption proclamation on 28 July 1868 and included all thirty states which had ratified. One could question the validity of the preamble (as well as its legal significance). It was not included anywhere in Seward's adoption proclamation. Its listing of only twenty-seven states, however, seems to lack consequence for the question of rescission, or for that matter, considering the resolution of concurrence, for the validity of the Fourteenth Amendment itself.

Arguments seeking to legitimate rescission point out the mootness of the question in this precedent, since by proclamation day Georgia had been counted, making twenty-eight states even without Ohio and New Jersey. But the real significance of the Fourteenth Amendment as precedent lies in the fact that Seward knew, upon presentation to the Congress on 20 July, that both rescinding states were needed to meet the legal requirements of adoption. Since he did not have the statutory authority to make the determination, he turned the problem over to the Congress, which decided in favor of adoption while ignoring Georgia's ratification. When Congress made its decision the question was not moot. Any mootness ensued only after the decision-making process was concluded by Congress. The conscious decision to ignore the withdrawals of New Jersey and Ohio is a powerful precedent.

Further congressional history follows this precedent. New York withdrew its ratification of the Fifteenth Amendment three months before its final adoption, yet was included in Secretary of State Fish's 30 March 1870 proclamation. During that three-month period Georgia once again ratified, eliminating the need for New York's inclusion. Fish, seeing no reason to submit the matter to Congress, proclaimed the adoption, noted New York's attempted withdrawal, but included it in the list of ratifying states. Interestingly, Roscoe Conkling noted on the Senate floor the futility of New York's attempt to undo its ratification: ''Its own recitals cancel it because they show that New York's approval of the great act of equality, which temporary majorities seek to destroy, has passed forever beyond their reach.'' His remark speaks eloquently to the treatment by subsequent Congresses of the Fourteenth Amendment precedent as controlling.

Similarly, an attempt by Tennessee to rescind ratification of the Nineteenth Amendment failed to eliminate its name from the 1920 adoption proclamation.

One other incident occurred during ratification of the Twenty-fifth Amendment (presidential succession) which began a comedy of errors. Attempting to gain the distinction of becoming the thirty-eighth state to ratify, North Dakota ratified one state too soon, and then, upon realizing its mistake, promptly attempted to withdraw its consent. Minnesota, aware of North Dakota's ratification but not its withdrawal, then ratified, assuming it had put the amendment over the top. Nevada's ratification followed immediately. There is no precedential value here since no North Dakota official had the opportunity to send notice of ratification to Washington and none was recorded. Does this actually make Nevada the thirty-eighth state? It would be hard to find a better example of the administrative confusion created by the possibility of rescission or of the mutual dependence of one state's action on those of other states, not to mention the inherent unfairness to relying states or their affected citizens.

Rescission proponents have maintained that the events connected with the Fourteenth and Fifteenth amendments have little precedential value since they were born of duress, fed by despair, and nutured by the bayonets of the Union army. They refer, of course, to the post–Civil War era when the Congress was largely controlled by a powerfully dedicated group of radical reconstructionists. No one could deny that Reconstruction was a particularly difficult period, and that the country suffered deep divisions. Yet the reasoning disregards the fact that many amendments have been the result of stressful times. Without more substantial evidence to buoy it, the argument could then logically be used by others to deny the precedents which arose from the 1920s, the Great Depression, and 1968. *Leser* v. *Garnett* addressed itself to such an assertion: "The suggestion that the Fifteenth was incorporated in the Constitution, not in accordance with law, but practically as a war measure which has been validated by acquiescence, cannot be entertained." Although reinstatement of congressional representation for some southern states depended upon ratification of the Fourteenth Amendment, neither New Jersey nor Ohio were so pressured, and it was their actions which were at issue and the basis of the legal precedent regarding rescission.

The "invalid because blackmailed" argument was used unsuccessfully in the courts in 1954. In *United States* v. *Gugel,* the court quickly dismissed the notion, relying simply upon the controlling line of cases holding that once notification of ratification is received from the final state required, adoption is binding upon the courts.

The first real litigation to arise from the Fourteenth Amendment rescission issue did not occur until 1964, in *Jackman* v. *Bodine*. The president of the New Jersey senate challenged an order of reapportionment, contending that since New Jersey had rescinded its ratification, the equal protection basis for reapportionment contained in that amendment was not applicable. Refusing to rule on historical evidence and indicating that one hundred years was too long a time to wait to litigate the issue, the court observed: "Plaintiffs dispute the factual premise, but we think it makes no difference whether New Jersey did or did not approve the Amendment." The issue surfaced again in *Maryland Petition Committee* v. *Johnson* in 1967. There, the federal district court held that the validity of ratification was solely a political question, to be decided only by Congress. It too cited the lateness of the hour for such a challenge to the Fourteenth Amendment and voided the issue for mootness.

Historical precedent, therefore, overwhelmingly tips the scales in opposition to rescission. Reasonable people may disagree over the significance to be attached to actions of Congress, since there is no congressional doctrine comparable to the *stare decisis* (reliance on precedent) of the precedent-oriented courtroom. Yet despite the truth of the argument that one legislative body cannot bind a subsequent one, parliamentary law relies heavily upon precedent, making it far from clear that rescissionists can safely ignore the history of past attempts. While Congress need not exhibit rigid consistency, it has nonetheless attempted over the years to assure the nation of some stability and rational predictability in its decision-making process—if only to maintain its own credibility. Congressional history, then, can be taken as a reasonably reliable guide to future action on the legality of rescission, barring a complete turnaround in public opinion, which seems unlikely. Congressional precedent is especially significant if one concludes that the issue of rescission is nonjusticiable—that it belongs not in the courts but in the political ballpark of the Congress.

Chapter 4

The Courts and the Constitution

Generally, the trend of case law examining amendment ratification shows a gradual retreat from rulings "on the merits" of cases to subtle flirtations with the "political question" doctrine, while, in fact, ruling only on procedural improprieties.

Ratification questions were brought to the courts as early as 1798. *Hollingsworth* v. *Virginia* held that the president need not approve the Eleventh Amendment (limiting the right of a noncitizen to sue a state). Its pertinence lies in the Supreme Court's ready assumption of jurisdiction without discussion and its narrow interpretation of Article V. The court, however, presumably had a greater interest in the Eleventh Amendment than in most, since it directly affected the power and jurisdiction of the judiciary and its adoption circumvented the 1793 decision in *Chisolm* v. *Georgia*, which allowed suit against a state by a citizen of another state in limited circumstances.

The precursor to modern case law was the Maine high court's decision, *In Re Opinion of the Justices* (1919), holding ratification final without resort to public vote. Here again the court opted for a narrow interpretation, refusing to read between the lines of Article V. In a succeeding case, *Hawke* v. *Smith,* the United States Supreme Court followed suit the next year.

The Supreme Court began to draw the fine line between ruling on the merits and ruling on procedure in an Eighteenth Amendment case, *Dillon* v. *Gloss,* in 1920. Charged with transporting liquor in violation of that recently enacted amendment, the defendant appealed, challenging the validity of the seven-year time limit set by Congress for adoption. Holding that as long as the length of time is reasonable the courts should refrain from interference with congressional designations, even in procedural areas, the court concluded:

Whether a definite period for ratification shall be fixed so that all may know what it is and speculation on what is a reasonable time may be avoided, is, in our opinion, a matter of detail which Congress may determine as an incident of its power to designate the mode of ratification.

With this case the court began a judicial withdrawal from substantive decisions on the ratification process.

In 1922, *Leser* v. *Garnett* refused to allow the states to establish internal procedures impinging on ratification by refusing to permit a second vote during the same session. Encroachment was similarly denied both the executive and judicial branches. Since the power to adopt the resolutions lay with the legislatures of West Virginia and Tennessee, "[o]fficial notice to the Secretary, duly authenticated, that they had done so, was conclusive upon him, and, being certified to by his proclamation, is conclusive upon the courts." The case appears to speak definitively to the questions both of the finality of ratification and of its nonjusticiability, since notice of such act is conclusive upon both the secretary and the courts. If ratification is so determinative, the *Leser* court leaves little room for rescission.

A case often cited by rescission advocates as contrary to the substantive holding in *Leser* is *Wise* v. *Chandler,* a 1937 decision of the Kentucky Court of Appeals upholding a challenge to ratification of the child labor amendment. In 1925, Kentucky had rejected that amendment. The lower court reasoned that the legislature then functioned solely as a ratifying convention, and therefore any action, including an initial rejection, was final. In effect, the court balanced the finality of rejection with the assumed finality of ratification. The Kentucky Court of Appeals, after relating the historical precedent of the Fourteenth Amendment and thereby recognizing the invalidity of rescission, found:

It is hardly consonant with common sense to say that an amendment, once proposed for ratification, could never be rejected. The very purpose of proposing an amendment must be to poll the sentiment of the various States on the question. It would be an anomaly if that sentiment could be expressed effectively in only one way. We can see no reason for attaching less dignity to the expression of the sovereign will of the State in rejecting an amendment than is attached to its action in ratifying such an amendment. It would be a singular thing to say that rejections are allowed, but when they occur they are to be treated as nonexistent.

Those alluding to this dictum on behalf of rescission attempts would appear to have misread the case. The court not only did not transpose rescission into rejection, but held that *either* a ratification or rejection was conclusive and not subject to change—even after the public had twelve years to reconsider.

That dictum was actually never approved on appeal by the Supreme Court, which avoided the issue and dismissed the case "on the ground that

after the Governor of Kentucky had forwarded certification of the ratification . . . to the Secretary of State of the United States there was no
longer a controversy susceptible of judicial determination.'' Justices Black
and Douglas concurred: ''[W]e do not believe that state or federal courts
have any jurisdiction to interfere with the amending process.'' Oddly, the
Supreme Court issued its opinion in *Wise* immediately following the famous
decision in *Coleman* v. *Miller* (1939), where it was, in effect, asserted that a
rejection was not a final act, unlike a ratification. Because both cases
presented the same question and were simultaneously decided, the holdings
cannot be considered contradictory. Although their impact on the factual
situations diverged (*Wise* treated rejection as a final act and *Coleman* did
not), their actual holdings are consistent. Both *Wise* and *Coleman* held that
the validity of a ratification is a nonjusticiable political question. Therefore,
reliance by rescissionists only on the Kentucky court's decision seems
shortsighted.

Commentators have long noted the gradual encroachment by the
courts into the political question arena. In *Sierra Club* v. *Morton,* even the
Supreme Court has observed, quoting the words of Alexis de Tocqueville,
that ''scarcely any political question arises in the United States that is not
resolved, sooner or later, into a judicial question.'' For some years now,
many scholars and government experts have decried the movement of the
courts into the area of the political question. Legislating, they claim, is for
legislative bodies and should be eschewed by the judiciary. Judicial law-
making is indeed a questionable practice, for it carries with it legal fiat in
interpreting political aspects of the Constitution or statute in place of the
responsibility of a legislative body to an electorate. Yet the truth is found in
the old cliché that nature abhors a vacuum. In fact, most examples of judicial
lawmaking have come about because congressmen and legislators have
found themselves unable or unwilling to act, and the courts have found
themselves unable to escape acting (although, in many cases, happily). The
proliferation of class actions and attempts on the part of litigants to force
constitutional decisions have made this inevitable. So too is it inevitable that
the question of rescission of constitutional ratifications should bring us face
to face with the question of whether the courts may invade the political area
surrounding the substance of the constitutional amending process.

Of all the cases on ratification, *Coleman* v. *Miller* (1939) is surely the
most widely debated. Some find its holding to be clear and unambiguous,
and attempts to dismiss it as inconclusive or inconsistent to be weak. Others,
noting it consisted of four opinions, none of which represented the majority
of the justices, claim it lacks precedential value. The case arose when

plaintiffs sought to prevent Kansas officials from sending notice of ratification of the child labor amendment to the secretary of state, using the argument of the *Wise* court in Kentucky that the legislature's prior rejection of the proposition was final and prevented later ratification. The Kansas Supreme Court rejected the plea and recognized the later ratification as final and complete. The state legislators who had previously rejected the amendment applied for a United States Supreme Court hearing.

The four opinions in that decision are still cloaked in controversy. The Opinion of the Court is controlling. It held that the Supreme Court did have jurisdiction to consider the matter, but that the issue of determining the validity of a ratification was a political question which congress alone had the authority to answer.

> We think that in accordance with this historic precedent the question of the efficacy of ratifications by state legislatures, in the light of previous rejection or attempted withdrawal, should be regarded as a political question pertaining to the political departments, with the ultimate authority in the Congress, in the exercise of its control over the promulgation of the adoption of the amendment.

Citing the historical precedents in confronting the issues of rescission and rejection, the Supreme Court concluded: "[T]he political departments of the Government dealt with the effect both of previous rejection and of attempted withdrawal and determined that both were ineffectual in the presence of an actual ratification." Senator Ervin, a leading rescissionist (and an unabashed opponent of ERA) points out that the opinion by Chief Justice Hughes and announced by Justice Stone was not a majority opinion, and that therefore their comments regarding rescission lack significance.

A close analysis, however, of the concurring opinion, written by Justice Black and joined by Justices Roberts, Frankfurter, and Douglas, discloses that they did not disagree in any way with the power of Congress to make the ultimate determination. Indeed, their opinion disagreed with that of Hughes and Stone only in part.

> To the extent that the Court's opinion in the present case even impliedly assumes a power to make judicial interpretation of the exclusive constitutional authority of Congress over submission and ratification of amendments, we are unable to agree.

"Therefore, judicial expression," wrote Black, "amounting to more than mere acknowledgment of exclusive Congressional power over the political process of amendment is a mere admonition to the Congress in the nature of an advisory opinion given wholly without constitutional authority."

The two dissenters, Justices Butler and McReynolds, found the thirteen-year delay in ratifying the proposed amendment to be beyond a reasonable time limit, according to the 1920 admonition set out in *Dillon* v. *Gloss.*

Several obvious conclusions may be drawn from *Coleman* v. *Miller* if some simple arithmetic is used on the positions of the justices. All but the two dissenters believed the issue was a political question; and all but the dissenters found the issue to be one for Congress, and therefore not justiciable, although the controlling opinion took jurisdiction in order to say so. Finally, none of the justices disagreed with the willingness of a clear majority to allow the decision of Congress to stand: a ratification is final and cannot be rescinded.

Critics of the *Coleman* decision have countered that the 1939 case has been superseded and to a great extent overruled by those subsequent cases in which the court did, in fact, enter into fields once considered the province of the legislative branch. Most frequently cited are the cases of *Powell* v. *McCormack* (1969, on the seating of a congressman), and *Baker* v. *Carr* (1962, the revolutionary decision on reapportionment). These and other recent cases have undeniably narrowed the restrictions imposed by the judiciary upon itself through the "political question" doctrine. But those eager to seize upon the trend should be aware that important distinctions exist. Never since the *Coleman* decision has the Supreme Court imposed its judgment upon the substantive determination of whether any given amendment should be adopted. The cases cited to assert the justiciable nature of political questions were decisions of the so-called Warren Court. It is dangerous to assume that the Burger Court will be as intrusive. Indeed, that court could well retreat from those positions.

It is pertinent that the *Powell* case, ruling on Adam Clayton Powell's seating in the House of Representatives, was not decided on his lack of constitutionally specified qualifications but on nonconstitutional grounds. This case demanded resolution on the basis of evidentiary decision making, a role for which the court was specially equipped and an obvious arbiter. To analogize the *Powell* case, therefore, to *Coleman*-type cases based on the constitutionally inspired amendment process leads to obvious problems based on the differences inherent in the two decisions. It does not follow that *Powell* would necessarily alter the doctrine on *Coleman*.

Baker v. *Carr* set the scene for an entire line of reapportionment cases which clearly moved into the area of political question answering, once strictly a legislative prerogative. *Reynolds* v. *Sims*, establishing the "one man, one vote" doctrine in 1964, is an outstanding example. Yet since judicial intervention comes about only when the legislature fails to meet the timely reapportionment required by the Constitution, it is also risky to analogize the reapportionment cases. *Butterworth* v. *Dempsey* said it in 1965: "Such determinations will be made when necessary, but only when the political branches fail to make them and then only to the extent necessary to enforce the plaintiffs' rights." This decision was echoed by *Moore* v. *Moore*, which disallowed nominating congressmen at large in lieu of redistricting. Thus it is the failure of the legislative body to act, and not its action, which imposes a burden upon the judiciary to interfere. Since courts allow intervention only upon a showing of improper or no legislative action, analogies between the *Baker*-inspired reapportionment cases and adoption of a constitutional amendment appear illogical. In this area Congress has acted clearly, determining in the past which ratifications are valid. This eliminates any need for the courts to act as long as Congress continues to exercise its political judgment over amendments.

The *Baker* case established six criteria for determining that a constitutional issue is nonjusticiable on political grounds. These criteria are: 1) a textually demonstrable constitutional commitment of an issue to a coordinate political department; 2) the lack of judicially discoverable and manageable standards for resolving it; 3) the impossibility of deciding without an initial policy determination, which determination is clearly for nonjudicial discretion; 4) the impossibility of a court making such a determination without expressing a lack of respect due coordinate branches of government; 5) an unusual need to adhere unquestionably to past political decisions; and 6) the potential of embarrassment caused by different pronouncements for various departments.

These criteria would appear to bar judicial review in determining the validity of ratifications. Courts have consistently held that Article V textually demonstrates a commitment of the amendment issue to Congress, whose decision is binding on the courts. Therefore the issue of rescinding could be considered a political question on the first criterion alone. Further, the courts have continued to show unquestioning adherence to and respect for congressional decisions, as set forth in the fifth criterion. Would not the rendering of a substantive decision on ratification constitute "a policy determination" (already in fact made by Congress) which would be clearly an expression of disrespect for that political branch? Constitutional amendments are in many instances proposed to circumvent or overrule court decisions. The Eleventh Amendment, the proposed antibusing and antiabortion amendments, and ERA itself are all examples. Only with difficulty can anyone argue the logic of permitting the same court the public is attempting to circumvent with an amendment the right to further veto public action taken for public benefit. If any area should be sacrosanct from judicial encroachment, it should be the adoption or ratification of constitutional amendments.

One must also consider the decision in *Vincent* v. *Schlesinger* (1975), in which a federal district court in Washington, D.C., cited *Baker* v. *Carr* in refusing to rule even on the procedures employed by President Ford's clemency program, which was instituted by proclamation, explaining that "such a determination is impossible to make 'without an initial policy determination of a kind clearly for non-judicial discretion.' " Therefore, whether the president intended the procedures followed is a political question. There is no reason not to afford the legislative branch the same respect.

Even in a case of greater concern to the judiciary, *Buchanan* v. *Rhodes* (1966), a federal district court refused to review the merits. Ohio's larger counties had decried a lack of equal protection in a statute guaranteeing each county at least one court of common pleas judge. "If," said the court, "we were to undertake an independent resolution of the question posed by this complaint, we would necessarily express a lack of respect for the bona fide attempts by the Ohio Legislature to increase the number of judges in urban counties to alleviate docket congestion." How can one argue that there should be less deference from the courts in the ratification of amendments than in the control they exercise over their own judicial brethren?

The *Baker* decision itself puts the issue of rescission at rest, even aside from the criteria it listed. "It is the relationship between the judiciary and the coordinate branches of the Federal Government, and not the federal judiciary's relationship to the States, which gives rise to the political question." Since all agree that states are performing a federal function sitting as ratifying conventions during the amendment process, the issue does not lie between the federal courts and the states per se. By virtue of the federal function leading to a congressional resolution adopting an amendment, any issue would be between the federal courts and the people represented by Congress, an interbranch dispute. Issues of federalism are subject to court determination. Courts, however, have fairly consistently refused to become the final arbiter of questions involving the separation of powers. Although questions between the states and the federal government may be susceptible of court determination, constitutional disputes over the amendment process must be looked at with extreme care before the courts will intervene.

Those critical of the foregoing analysis cite the 1975 case of *Dyer* v.

Blair, which allowed the Illinois legislature to determine that a three-fifths vote is required to pass a ratification resolution. On this basis they argue that the courts will in fact interfere in such questions. The essential part of the federal court's holding in *Dyer* was the determination that the issue was justiciable because Article V did not expressly prescribe a majority vote.

> We think the omission more reasonably indicates that the framers intended to treat the determination of the vote required to pass a ratifying resolution as an aspect of the process that each state legislature, or state convention, may specify for itself.

The key word "process," read against the background of other cases, suggests that the courts will review only procedural aspects of ratification arising prior to the receipt of notice by the Administrator of General Services—that is, aspects of the internal, procedural functioning of a state legislature prior to the vote. Indeed, the court voiced a doubt it would assent to review any challenge, once notice of ratification was received, that the procedures adopted were not followed. Viewed in this light, what at first blush is an anomaly offers no departure from the line of cases discussing ratification which allow review of procedural provisions like referenda and the reasonableness of the time period for ratification. Again, it may appear that *Dyer* is a departure from the landmark case of *Leser* v. *Garnett*, but that case refused to allow restrictive procedures which would *prevent* a vote. The facts in *Dyer* were based on procedures *for* voting, and thus can be distinguished on a positive rather than negative basis.

Dyer v. *Blair*, written by now Supreme Court Justice John Paul Stevens, is also consistent with preceding cases in its narrow interpretation of Article V. "If the framers had intended to require the state legislatures to act by simple majority, we think they would have said so explicitly." *Hawke* v. *Smith* put it similarly. "The language of the article is plain, and admits of no doubt in its interpretation. It is not the function of courts or legislative bodies, national or state, to alter the method which the Constitution has fixed." That language of the United States Supreme Court would appear to be the ultimate in strict constructionism—a doctrine leaving little room for the constitutionally unmentioned question of rescission.

Chapter 5

The Fate of ERA and Rescission

It is doubtful, although not impossible, that litigation contesting the validity of rescission will occur prior to ratification of ERA by the required number of states. If thirty-eight states have not ratified by the deadline there will be no issue to decide; the question will have become moot. The Tennessee Supreme Court has already held that the judiciary cannot intervene during the ratification processes (*Clements* v. *Roberts*, 1920). While that decision would appear to be contrary to the *Dyer* case, the Tennessee court made it clear in *Walker* v. *Dunn* (1972) that courts can review procedural matters after adoption. The move from substantive to procedural review would seem to have taken hold.

Who has standing to sue? Although Idaho legislators have suggested that that state's attorney general should initiate a suit on behalf of its secretary of state, the authorities appear to be in agreement. In the *Maryland Petition* case a federal district court determined that "standing" to bring a declaratory judgment to nullify a ratification required that the plaintiff have a greater and more particularized concern with the subject than does the general public. Existing federal precedent has led to the suggestion that a female legislator who voted for rescission has a special interest and therefore standing to sue. But the amendment will best be tested by a citizen subject to discrimination when the amendment is effective two years after adoption. The defense to such a suit by the official charged with enforcement will be the invalidity of the adoption.

Speculating on what the Supreme Court will do is a favorite but chancy pastime. Yet the Burger Court's record of judicial restraint, coupled with its penchant for strict construction, should give little comfort to the forces favoring rescission. Let's assume the court did find the issue justiciable. If the court decided the issue on its merits, its tendency for strict construction—which would mean a narrow construction of Article V—along with the considerable authority negating rescission (as opposed to a mere paucity of contrary precedent)—seem likely to result in the final nullification of rescission as a viable doctrine. As Raymond Planell put it in the *Notre Dame Lawyer* (February 1974):

> The law is clearly on the side of those in favor of the amendment; any suits should produce a nullification of rescissions and, consequently, cause states to consider the merits of amendments more astutely before undertaking the irrevocable act of ratification (p. 670).

But will the court intervene? The probability is that its tendency toward restraint will continue to prevail and that it will not. Charles Black, Yale Law School's constitutional scholar, indicates, while expressing his disagreement with it, that *Coleman* may imply that rescission is a political question. Our feeling is that the court probably will opt for the political question doctrine, and that the final verdict will be in favor of the nonjusticiability of the question, based on the Fourteenth Amendment—*Coleman* line of reasoning. If the court does consider the validity of constitutional amendments to be a nonjusticiable political question, then Congress is once again in the position to be the sole judge.

Hasty predictions about any legislative branch, subject as they are to both political and nonpolitical lobbying pressures, has left many an "expert" prematurely gray. Yet Congress has, in the recent past, exhibited enough consistency to allow the accurate vote counter the luxury of making some reasonably reliable guesses. Considering its makeup, the predisposition of the present occupant of the White House, the overwhelming vote on the original congressional ERA proposal, and the lack of desire to flip-flop (and thus alienate both sides engaged in the argument), the bet here is that Congress will find that it has no choice and will follow the congressional precedent set during the experiences of the Fourteenth and Fifteenth Amendments.

Probably some legal opinions are clouded by a political predisposition, subconscious or otherwise, toward ERA itself. If this is true, it is reasonable to expect that some who hold one position on rescission where ERA is concerned may gravitate to the opposite direction on a "right to life" amendment attempting to circumvent the Supreme Court's position on abortion. This vacillation would contribute toward leaving the process of adopting constitutional amendments, one of democracy's most sensitive, serious, and unretractable acts, firmly in the political arena, where the founding fathers appear to have intended it to reside.

Most of the controversy surrounding rescission would in fact be eliminated if Congress stood up to its responsibility and acted now. A detailed statute setting forth the procedures involved in ratification and rescission is not only in order but a valid exercise of the legislative power of

Congress pursuant to Article V. Long overdue, it is a recommendation the legislative branch should not dismiss out of hand. There is sufficient precedent, clearly an approaching problem, and every reason to desire to prevent a pending constitutional crisis, of whatever magnitude. The federal system would be well served by forthright legislative behavior which once and for all puts this adoption issue to rest.

What is the most logical legislative response for Congress? The heavy weight of history and the need to avoid administrative confusion lead inevitably to the conclusion that finality is not only desirable but necessary when considering ratification of an amendment. Since the same is not necessarily true of rejection, Congress ought to make clear that ratification, once taken, is final. This step alone will help ensure that amendment decisions are not taken lightly, and only after the considerable deliberation they deserve. Realistically, is it likely that Congress will act? Probably not. Politicians rarely take what they consider unnecessary actions. After all, proponents of ERA may fail to get the required three states and the issue of rescission will silently disappear. Many legislators will also see rescission legislation as a "no win" issue because of the furor whipped up over ERA. What lesson is to be learned from this situation?

The questions surrounding rescission transcend the issue itself. Public recognition of the facts involved—and more important, of the questions needed to be asked—form an integral part of what may be the most significant aspect of the kind of government the framers envisaged. We clearly need to know more about the kinds of behavioral patterns exhibited by congressmen and legislators alike—those people who woo us for our vote, but to whom we need not be irrevocably wed. Congressional behavior, like that of the state legislatures, merits a closer look. The right answers can come only when we ask the right questions of our government.

Many factors underlie the movement toward rescission, some of them partly obscured by the polarization of responses to ERA. Perhaps the most formidable is the growing desire of persons at the state level for increased states' rights. Those persons often point to section two of the proposed amendment, that giving Congress the power to enforce the amendment by appropriate legislation. This, they argue, is an open invitation to the federal government to impinge on state power and further increase government centralization. The provision is a copy of powers given to Congress in many previous amendments.

The 1970s have produced increases in revenue sharing and presidential vetoes. Party loyalties are being displaced by regional concerns and growing state antagonism to the federal bureaucracy. All have fostered the desire of state officials to keep policy making close to home. Their desire for local autonomy appears to be trickling down to the electorate. Even the underlying issue of states' rights can reasonably be classified as a political question. Congress, by virtue of its constitutionally mandated supremacy, can best decide such a question since it is not overly influenced by interests controlling the state capitols. In an era characterized by a particular sensitivity on the part of legislative and judicial bodies to the rights of individuals, the Congress could well seize upon ERA as an opportunity to regain its legislative supremacy.

As a nation come swiftly to adulthood, we have arrived at a time requiring our acceptance of political accountability for what are actually our own political decisions. For years we have used (and misused) legal institutions and legal doctrine to reach desired political goals, often couching them in the language of the courtroom. Interpretation of the law in hazy or unclear areas is a risky business, and all the more so with constitutional doctrine. There are scholars who surely believe the Constitution permits rescission. There are many who just as surely do not. In truth, the Constitution is silent on the subject, and precious little exists in the constitutional debates to ensure definitive consideration. We are dealing, therefore, with probabilities.

The debate will be politically motivated and decided, cloaked though it may be in legal language. There is nothing necessarily wrong with this. We need not continually rely on experts to order our lives. Congress will act only if the public insists upon it. A court decision is no more sacrosanct than a congressional decision. Those most affected are capable of making their own decisions and accepting responsibility for them.

Recent Developments

On 15 August 1978, the House approved H.J. Res. 638, which extended the deadline for ratification of the ERA to 30 June 1982. The House also defeated an amendment offered by Mr. Railsback forcing the Administrator of General Services to certify all rescissions occurring prior to the original deadline, though recognizing that the final determination of adoption was up to Congress. That amendment was defeated by a vote of 196–227, with 9 abstentions. (See 124 *Cong. Rec.*, H8639, H8658 [daily ed. 15 August 1978].) At the time of this writing, the Senate has not acted, thereby leaving the House rejection of rescission attempts as the most recent expression of Congress.

For further materials, see H.R. Rep. No. 95–1405, 95th Cong., 2nd Sess. (1978); *Extending the Ratification Period for the Proposed Equal Rights Amendment, Hearings on H.J. Res. 638 before the Subcommittee on Civil and Constitutional Rights of the House Subcommittee on the Judiciary,* 95th Cong., 2nd Sess. (1978); and *The ERA Extension of Ratification Period, Hearings on S.J. Res. 134 before the Subcommittee on the Constitution of the Senate Committee on the Judiciary,* 95th Cong., 2nd Sess. (August 2–, 1978).

Appendices

Appendix A

Opinions of the State Attorneys General

1. Nebraska

On 16 February 1973, Attorney General Clarence Meyer, acting by Assistant Attorney General Calvin Robinson, issued Opinion No. 13, generally addressing the question of the resolution rescinding Nebraska's ratification of the ERA. This is the only opinion on the subject by that office. The following excerpts are from a letter addressed to State Senator Richard F. Proud.

> You ask, where the Legislature's ratification of a proposed amendment to the Constitution of the United States has been certified to the Administrator of General Services, whether such purported ratification would be voided by the fact that in passing the resolution, the Legislature allegedly failed to follow procedures provided.

It appeared that neither resolution purporting to ratify the ERA was printed prior to the vote as required by the constitution of Nebraska. However, the opinion found that certification of the ratification had been made.

After recognizing the holdings in *Leser* v. *Garnett* and *U.S. ex rel Widenmann* v. *Colby* that notice of ratification to the secretary of state is conclusive and the ruling of *Chandler* v. *Wise* that the court lacked jurisdiction to pass on the ratification question, the attorney general concluded:

> In summary of the above authorities, we are doubtful that alleged procedural defects, although constitutional in nature, can be raised either in the courts or before the Administrator of General Services, to challenge a certification of ratification. We know of no authority, either statutory or otherwise, which would indicate whether alleged procedural defects can be considered by Congress in its general supervision of the amendment process.

2. Tennessee

On 13 March 1973, Assistant Attorney General Robert H. Roberts responded to a query from State Representative Victor H. Ashe. The following excerpt is from his letter.

You have asked this office for an opinion as to whether this General Assembly may rescind the action of the previous General Assembly in ratifying the proposed amendment to the Federal Constitution. It is my opinion that this cannot be done.

It has been held by the United States Supreme Court and by our state Supreme Court that when the General Assembly acts on an amendment to the Federal Constitution it does so by virtue of the Federal Constitution, and its power is from that source. The 87th General Assembly acted on this question. Its action was certified to the appropriate federal authorities. This state is now on record as approving the amendment. It is my opinion that this action is irrevocable.

On 28 February 1977, James J. Mynatt, acting director of the Tennessee Legislative Council Committee, sent an explanatory letter to Samuel S. Freedman. The following excerpt is from that letter.

[T]he General Assembly's adoption in 1974 of Senate Joint Resolution 29, repealing House Joint Resolution 371 of 1972 and rescinding the earlier ratification of the Twenty-seventh Amendment, was surrounded by controversy.

Many eminent constitutional authorities (self-ordained and otherwise) were arrayed on both sides of the question as to whether or not the General Assembly had the legal authority to rescind or repeal or otherwise nullify or negate solemn acts of ratification once duly made.

The state attorney general was of the opinion that any rescission action would be invalid, but the General Assembly went ahead and did it anyway. The prevailing legal opinion seems to be that it is up to the Congress to decide how it shall treat such rescission actions—to observe or ignore them.

The ratification resolution was adopted by the House in 1972 by a vote of 72–0 and the Senate concurred by a vote of 25–5. The rescission resolution was barely adopted by the Senate, 18–11, with one present and not voting. (It takes 17 votes to pass or adopt in the Senate.) The vote was also close in the House—56–33. (It takes 50 votes to pass or adopt in the House.)

A major argument of the pro-rescission forces was that the earlier action was taken too quickly, without sufficient thought or debate and all the ramifications had not been fully considered.

3. Idaho

On 27 January 1975, Attorney General Wayne L. Kidwell responded to an inquiry by State Representatives C. L. Otter and Ralph J. Gines concerning an official opinion of the state attorney general of 24 January

1973 (No. 73–116), which stated that the Idaho legislature had no jurisdiction to retract its prior ratification of ERA.

> We believe that the former opinion went further in interpreting the law than legal authority would permit. The Idaho Legislature has the *power* to rescind its prior ratification of the E.R.A., although the *right* to rescind will ultimately be judged by the United States Congress in the exercise of its control over the promulgation of the adoption of the amendment.

On 12 February 1975, Attorney General Kidwell wrote to State Senator Edith Miller Klein in what was not an official opinion, but rather a letter intended "to provide legal guidance."

> I am pleased to respond to your letter of January 29, 1975, in which you have inquired whether the United States Congress has ever recognized the recision by a state legislature of its prior ratification of a proposed amendment to the United States Constitution. Your question must be answered in the negative. . . . While Congress has never recognized the attempted retraction of a ratification, and while Congress would most likely follow its own precedent in this matter, we feel, nevertheless, that the exercise of the power of recision is not a totally useless gesture, because it would at least give the Idaho Legislature standing to argue its case to the United States Congress and possibly the courts. We recognize that the United States Supreme Court expressly stated in 1938 that the promulgation of a constitutional amendment is a political question upon which the courts have no jurisdiction (*Coleman* v. *Miller*) . . . although it is equally true that the definition of a "political question" has undergone considerable change since 1938.

4. West Virginia

Attorney General Chauncey H. Browning, Jr., issued an opinion letter on 4 April 1973 to Howard D. Kenney, assistant director of the West Virginia Human Rights Commission, regarding the validity of rescission. This opinion was considered by the attorney general of Tennessee.

Attorney General Browning wrote: "The courts have been unanimous in holding that neither the Congress nor the legislatures in the several states are acting in a purely legislative manner with reference to their actions on proposed amendments to the Federal Constitution." After reviewing at length the major cases on rescission, he concluded that the Supreme Court, with its decision in *Leser* v. *Garnett,* "began to abdicate its jurisdiction in cases involving the finality or propriety of actions by the states in ratifying or rejecting proposed amendments to the Federal Constitution." He continued:

> A number of constitutional authorities and text writers, as well as some courts, conclude that ratification or rejection action by a legislature can be taken

but once, at which time the legislature exhausts all of its authority and legal ability to act on that issue until it is resubmitted by Congress.

It is apparent, however, that with respect to an indeterminate number of proposed amendments to the Federal Constitution, many states in the past have rescinded and reversed their earlier positions on the ratification question.

It also appears evident that the Congress of the United States has on occasion accepted or rejected attempts by state legislatures to change their position on the question of ratification or rejection depending upon whether such changes were necessary to complete the list of states required for ratification.

Another significant issue not examined in depth during the course of this opinion relates to the authority of a state to rescind or reverse its position on the question of ratification if in fact more than one fourth of the legislatures of the states have already certified their rejection of the proposed amendment. Of course, if a state may rescind or reverse its position on the ratification issue, then, who is to say with certainty that more than one fourth of the states have "finally" rejected the proposal?

On the basis of the cases cited hereinabove, and the less than lucid arguments and decisions contained therein, I am of the opinion that your question should be answered in the affirmative. It is my opinion that the West Virginia Legislature, before action is taken either (1) by three fourths of the state legislatures ratifying the proposed amendment, or (2) by one fourth of the state legislatures rejecting the proposed amendment, may rescind, reaffirm or reverse its current position of ratification.

Appendix B

Opinions of the U.S. Department of Justice and the Senate Committee on the Judiciary

1. Excerpt on Rescission from Brief on Extension of the Time Period for Ratification

On 31 October 1977, Assistant Attorney General John M. Harmon of the Office of Legal Counsel, Department of Justice, submitted a memorandum to Robert J. Lipshutz, counsel to the president, concerning the constitutionality of extending the time period allowable for the ratification of ERA. The following excerpt is from that memorandum, pp. 28–51. The original footnotes follow the text.

IV. The Possible Effect of H.J. Res. 638 on the Power of States to Rescind Prior Ratifications

A separate question raised by H.J. Res. 638 is whether an extension of the time period available for ratification by the States would empower them to rescind prior ratifications during the extension period. This question could conceivably arise in one of two situations. First, under the joint resolution as presently drafted, the question would be whether an extension without more [legislative guidance on the validity of rescission] would somehow trigger a right of rescission derived from Art. V itself. Second, were H.J. Res. 638 amended specifically to confer a right of rescission on the States, would it be constitutional[?]

We assume for the purposes of addressing these questions that if a State having ratified an amendment could constitutionally rescind that ratification during the initial seven-year period, that power would continue unabated through any extension period that might be adopted. Thus, the rescission question raised by H.J. Res. 638 might conveniently be cast as whether, assuming States may not rescind during the initial seven-year period, may they nevertheless be constitutionally empowered to do so (1) by virtue of Art. V or (2) congressional action taken pursuant to Art. V?

Because we think that the answer to these questions is dependent to a great extent on the resolution of whether States may rescind during the initial seven-year period, we turn first to that question.

The text of Art. V itself provides no conclusive answer to whether States may rescind their ratification of a proposed amendment prior to its being ratified by three-fourths of the States.[35] It will be noted that Art. V does speak only in positive terms of ratification of a proposed amendment, giving the States the power to ratify a proposed amendment but not the power to reject. Thus, as a textual matter, it is arguable that only affirmative acts taken in the proposal or ratification process have any constitutional significance and that such acts are to be regarded as final. *See* Burdick, *Law of the American Constitution, supra,* at 43.

The sole expression we have been able to find regarding the probable intent of the Framers on this question is that of James Madison. During the ratification debates in the State of New York, it had been suggested that New York ratify the Constitution on the condition that certain amendments proposed by the New York Convention would be adopted.[36] Alexander Hamilton, who objected to such a conditional ratification, sought Madison's views. Madison's reply was made in a letter[37] . . .in which he stated that

> The Constitution requires an adoption *in toto* and *for ever*. It has been so adopted by the other States. An adoption for a limited time would be as defective as an adoption of some of the articles only. In short any *condition* whatever must viciate the ratification.

Although this statement was made with regard to Art. VII of the Constitution, which required ratification by nine of the States to "establish" the Constitution among those States, we see nothing to suggest that Madison's reasoning should not be applied with equal force to proposed constitutional amendments. Perhaps more importantly, an examination of the history of ratification of the Constitution and amendments thereto demonstrates uniform application and general acceptance of this position taken by Madison—ratification must be unconditional and irrevocable.

A. The Historical Acceptance of Madison's Principle

The New York Convention, after rejecting a proposal to ratify the Constitution conditionally, ratified the Constitution, substituting the words "fullest confidence" for the words "on condition." II J. Elliot's Debates 411–13 (1854).[38]

During this early period it was also recognized that a State, after having refused to ratify the Constitution, could thereafter ratify it. Thus,

North Carolina's ratification of the Constitution in 1789 was taken as proper even though it had "rejected" the Constitution in 1788. *See* Warren, *The Making of the Constitution* 820 (1928). This principle was shortly thereafter extended to the Art. V amendment process when Pennsylvania ratified a proposed (but never adopted) amendment in 1791 after having refused to ratify it in 1790.[39] The available records of the Second Congress indicate that there was no comment whatsoever regarding Pennsylvania's actions when notice of it was transmitted to the Senate by President Washington. *See* 3 Annals of Congress 15 (1791).

Thus, from an early date in our constitutional history it appears to have been accepted that the act of ratification, once taken by a State, was final and that States could ratify amendments after having "rejected" them.

These questions were not raised again until the Civil War Amendments were going through the ratification process. The first of these, the Thirteenth Amendment, had been "rejected" by the Kentucky legislature in 1865 by a resolution then presented to the Governor by the legislature. Although he took the position that the resolution did not require his assent,[40] he commented on the resolution as follows:

> Rejection by the present Legislative Assembly only remits the question to the people and the succeeding legislature. Rejection no more precludes future ratification than refusal to adopt any other measure would preclude the action of your successors. When ratified by the legislatures of three-fourths of the several States, the question will be finally withdrawn, and not before. Until ratified it will remain an open question for the ratification of the legislatures of the several States. When ratified by the legislature of a State, it will be final as to such State; and, when ratified by the legislatures of three-fourths of the several states, will be final as to all. Nothing but ratification forecloses the right of action. When ratified all power is expended. Until ratified the right to ratify remains.[41]

Both the rescission and subsequent ratification questions were presented together in connection with the ratification of the Fourteenth Amendment. By the middle of July, 1868, twenty-nine States had ratified that amendment. At that time there were thirty-seven States, twenty-eight thus constituting the majority of three-quarters required by the Constitution. However, two of those twenty-nine States, North and South Carolina, previously failed to ratify it and then reversed themselves;[42] in two others, Ohio and New Jersey, the legislatures had passed resolutions withdrawing their prior ratification of the Amendment. On July 8, 1868, the Senate adopted a resolution requesting the Secretary of State to transmit to the Senate a list of the States whose legislatures had adopted the Amendment. 81 Cong. Globe 3857 (1868). On July 15, 1868, the President transmitted to the Senate the report of the Secretary of State in compliance with that resolution. The report drew attention to the resolutions of the legislatures of

New Jersey and Ohio purporting to withdraw their ratifications. *Id.*, at 4070. On July 18, 1868, Senator Sherman introduced a Joint Resolution declaring that the Fourteenth Amendment had been ratified. *Id.*, at 4197.

Two days later, July 20, 1868, Secretary of State Seward published a document in which he recited by name the 29 States which had ratified the Amendment, including those which had sought to revoke their ratification and those which originally had rejected it. 15 Stat. 706. With respect to New Jersey and Ohio, he observed:

> And whereas it further appears from official documents on file in this Department that the legislatures of two of the States first above enumerated, to wit, Ohio and New Jersey, have since passed resolutions respectively withdrawing the consent of each of said States to the aforesaid amendment; and whereas it is deemed a matter of doubt and uncertainty whether such resolutions are not irregular, invalid, and therefore ineffectual for withdrawing the consent of the said two States, or of either of them, to the aforesaid amendment. . . .

He then certified that

> if the resolutions of the legislatures of Ohio and New Jersey ratifying the aforesaid amendment are to be deemed as remaining of full force and effect, notwithstanding the subsequent resolutions of the legislatures of those States, which purport to withdraw the consent of said States from such ratification, then the aforesaid amendment has been ratified in the manner hereinbefore mentioned, and so has become valid, to all intents and purposes, as a part of the Constitution of the United States.

He thus indicated that the effectiveness of the amendment was contingent on the power of the State legislatures to withdraw their consent from the ratification.

The following day, July 21, 1868, Congress adopted the Sherman resolution, *supra,* as a concurrent resolution not presented to the President.[43] 81 Cong. Globe 4266, 4295–96 (1868). That resolution stated that whereas the Fourteenth Amendment had been ratified by the legislatures of 29 States, counting among them North Carolina, South Carolina, New Jersey, and Ohio, the Amendment was "hereby declared to be a part of the Constitution of the United States and it shall be duly promulgated as such by the Secretary of State."

On the same day, Georgia, which previously had rejected the Amendment, ratified it. 15 Stat. 708. Rumors, the authenticity of which were questioned, of that ratification reached the House of Representatives during its deliberation on the Sherman resolution. In view of the questionable nature of that information, the House did not amend the resolution so as to include Georgia among the ratifying States. 81 Cong. Globe 4296 (1818).

On July 28, 1868, Secretary Seward, in compliance with the Sherman resolution, unconditionally certified that the Fourteenth Amendment had become valid to all intents and purposes as a part of the Constitution of the United States. 15 Stat. 708. He listed New Jersey, Ohio, Georgia, and the two Carolinas among the ratifying States.

As the result of the ratification of the Amendment by Georgia, it had been approved by twenty-eight, *i.e.,* the requisite number of States, even if New Jersey and Ohio were disregarded. This consideration, however, did not render the congressional determination academic. First, the congressional decision must be read in the light of the situation which existed when it was made. At that time, Congress had not received official notice of Georgia's ratification of the amendment. Therefore, the ratifications of New Jersey and Ohio were necessary to carry it. Secondly, it should also be noted that the adoption of the Amendment required not only the inclusion of the States which had adopted the amendment and then sought to repudiate their ratification (New Jersey and Ohio), but also that of the States which first had rejected the Amendment and then ratified it (North and South Carolina, and subsequently Georgia). The Fourteenth Amendment thus could not have been adopted without the ratifications of States which originally had rejected it.

The adoption of the Fifteenth Amendment involved problems analogous to those which arose on the occasion of the adoption of the Fourteenth Amendment. In this case, however, the Amendment was published and certified by the Secretary of State without congressional guidance.

By the middle of February, 1870, the Fifteenth Amendment had been ratified by 30 States, one more than the required number. Two of them, however, Ohio and Georgia, had originally rejected it. Mathews, *Legislative and Judicial History of the Fifteenth Amendment* 65–67 & n. 45 (1909). Also, New York rescinded its ratification in January, 1870. The amendment therefore could be considered adopted only if the States which first had rejected it were counted or if the rescission by New York were considered to be without effect.

Congress was aware of these problems but was unable to take any action on them.[44] Thus, the New York resolutions rescinding the ratification of the Amendment were referred by the Senate to the Committee on the Revision of the Laws on January 11, 1870. 88 Cong. Globe 377 (1870). The Committee reported back on February 22, 1870, with the recommendation that the New York resolutions be indefinitely postponed. A spectacular debate ensued between Senator Conkling of New York and Senator Davis of Kentucky, 89 Cong. Globe 1477–81 (1870), but it does not appear that the Senate took any action on the report. On February 21, 1870, a resolution was introduced in the Senate declaring that the Fifteenth Amendment had become valid. The resolution was referred to a Committee, *id.*, at 1444. The Committee submitted its report on April 18, 90 Cong. Globe 2738 (1870) and the resolution was passed over on the motion of its sponsor, 91 Cong. Globe 3124 (1870). On March 3, 1870, the Senate adopted a resolution requesting the Secretary of State to advise it of the States which had ratified the Amendment, 89 Cong. Globe 1653 (1870). The response from the Secretary is unknown.

Finally, on March 30, 1870, President Grant sent Congress a message advising it of the promulgation of the Fifteenth Amendment by the Secretary of State. 90 Cong. Globe 2298 (1870). The certificate of the Secretary of State, 16 Stat. 1131, listed twenty-nine States, including Ohio and New York but excluding Georgia, as having ratified the Amendment, and continued.

> And, further, that the States whose legislatures have so ratified the said proposed amendment constitute three-fourths of the whole number of States in the United States.
> And further, that it appears from an official document on file in this Department that the legislature of the State of New York has since passed resolutions claiming to withdraw the said ratification of the said amendment which had been made by the legislature of that State, and of which official notice had been filed in this Department.
> And, further, that it appears from an official document on file in this Department that the legislature of Georgia has by resolution ratified the said proposed amendment. . . .

The statement ''that the States whose legislatures have so ratified the said proposed amendment constitute three-fourths of the whole number of States'' tends to indicate that the Secretary of State did not recognize the withdrawal of New York to have been effective. The separate enumeration of Georgia seems to have served the same purpose, because the ratification of New York would not have been required if Georgia had been included in the list of ratifying States. The separate listing of Georgia could not have been due to last minute ratification by that State. The proclamation was dated March 30, 1870. Georgia had ratified the Amendment on February 2, 1870, followed by Iowa (February 3, 1870), Nebraska (February 17, 1870), and Texas (February 18, 1870). *See* U.S.C.A. Constitution, Amendment XV, Historical Note. The last three States were included in the first list of ratifying States.

The House of Representatives signified its approval of the promulgation of the Fifteenth (and Fourteenth) Amendment by adopting on July 11, 1870, a resolution to the effect that the amendment had become valid as a part of the Constitution. 93 Cong. Globe 5441 (1870).[45] No similar action was taken in the Senate, except, of course, for its later adoption of legislation implementing the Amendment.

The only pertinent judicial announcement of that period is a dictum in *White* v. *Hart,* 13 Wall. 646, 649 (1871) to the effect that the validity of the adoption of the Fourteenth and Fifteenth Amendments by Georgia was a political question not subject to judicial scrutiny. The Court said:

> Upon the same grounds she might deny the validity of her ratification of the constitutional amendments. The action of Congress upon the subject cannot be inquired into. The case is clearly one in which the judicial is bound to follow the action of the political department of the government, and is concluded by it (citing *Luther* v. *Borden,* 7 Howard, 43, 47, 57; *Rose* v. *Himely,* 4 Cranch 272; *Gelston* v. *Hoyt,* 3 Wheaton, 324 *Id.* 634; *Williams* v. *The Suffolk Ins. Co.,* 13 Peters, 420).

The issue whether a State can change the position by its legislature with respect to a constitutional amendment also arose in various degrees in connection with the adoption of the Sixteenth, Eighteenth, and Nineteenth Amendments. In none of these instances did the Secretary of State refer the matter to Congress.

Arkansas, which originally had rejected the Sixteenth Amendment, subsequently ratified it. The certificate of the Secretary of State lists Arkansas without comment among the ratifying States. 37 Stat. (Pt. II) 1785. It is, however, not apparent whether the approval of that State was required to obtain the necessary number of ratifications. S. Doc. 314, 76th Cong., 3d Sess. 25 (1940).

The issue whether ratification by the State legislature was final arose indirectly in connection with an attempt in Maine to subject the ratification of the Eighteenth Amendment by the State legislature to the State's initiative and referendum procedures. The Maine Supreme Court held that the amendment could not be subjected to a referendum. *Opinion of the Justices,* 118 Me. 544 (1919). One of the reasons for the decision was the consideration that, under the precedents established in connection with the adoption of the Fourteenth and Fifteenth Amendments, the legislation ratifying an amendment was final and could not be rescinded. *Id.,* at 548–49.[46]

The Nineteenth Amendment was ratified by the State of Tennessee on August 18, 1920. On August 26, 1920, the Secretary of State issued his certificate declaring that the amendment had been adopted by the required number of States, including Tennessee, 41 Stat. (Pt. II) 1823. Five days later, the Tennessee legislature sought to rescind the resolution adopting the amendment on the ground that it had been approved in the absence of a quorum and in violation of constitutional procedural safeguards. The

Secretary of State disregarded the resolution of rescission. *See* 65 *Cong. Rec.* 4491–92 (1924) (Remarks of Sen. Wadsworth); *Clements* v. *Roberts,* 144 Tenn. 129 (1920); *Leser* v. *Board of Registry,* 139 Md. 46, 71–73 (1921), *aff'd sub. nom. Leser* v. *Garnett,* 258 U.S. 130, 137 (1922).

Thereafter, Senator Wadsworth of New York and Congressman Garrett of Tennessee introduced an amendment to Article V of the Constitution. The part of that proposal pertinent here would have provided that

until three-fourths of the States have ratified or more than one-fourth of the States have rejected or defeated a proposed amendment, any State may change its vote.[47]

The proposal thus would have overturned by constitutional amendment the rule postulated by Madison and established in connection with the Civil War Amendments by enabling a State to rescind its ratification of an amendment until the time when the amendment becomes effective; and by preventing a State which had rejected an amendment from changing its position once more than a quarter of the States had rejected the amendment.

Both sponsors of the proposal conceded that these provisions were contrary to existing law; indeed both conceded that their proposals were designed to remedy what they considered to be a defect in the Constitution. . . .The Wadsworth-Garrett proposal apparently never got to a vote in either House.

The question whether a State can change a position taken with respect to a constitutional amendment arose again in connection with the Child Labor Amendment. That amendment had been submitted to the States in 1924. In the following year it appeared that more than one-fourth of the States had affirmatively rejected it. Congressman Garrett thereupon introduced a resolution which would have required the Secretary of State to report to Congress the action reported to him by the States regarding the amendment. 67 Cong. Rec. 576 (1925). Supporters of the amendment opposed the resolution because they feared that it was designed to lay the foundation for the claim that the amendment had been irretrievably defeated. *Id.,* at 1505–06 (1926). Congressman Garrett stated, *id.,* at 1506, that he had

no doubt that it is within the power of the legislature of any State that has acted on the amendment adversely to reconsider its action and act favorably, if it chooses to do so within the next year or two, for I imagine the Supreme Court would hold that was within a reasonable time.[48]

The resolution passed, *id.,* at 1507, and the Secretary of State submitted his report on February 9, 1926, which indicated that the amendment had been ratified in 4 States, affirmatively rejected in 13, failed ratification in both Houses in 3, and that some adverse action had been taken in some form by one House in 6 States. *Id.*, at 3801. No action was taken on that report.

The tide turned, however, in the 1930's, when an ever-increasing number of States, including many who had previously rejected the amendment, began to ratify it.[49] The question whether a State could ratify the amendment after its legislature had once rejected it was subsequently presented in *Coleman* v. *Miller*, 307 U.S. 433 (1939), and its companion case, *Chandler* v. *Wise*, 307 U.S. 474 (1939).

In 1925, the Kansas Legislature rejected the Child Labor Amendment and sent a certified copy of that action to the United States Secretary of State. In 1937, the Kansas Legislature adopted a resolution ratifying the amendment by a vote of 21–20, with the Lieutenant Governor casting the decisive vote. Several outvoted Kansas legislators thereupon instituted mandamus proceedings against the Secretary of the State Senate designed to prevent the ratification resolution from becoming effective. The complaint was based, *inter alia*, on the arguments (a) that the State of Kansas had once rejected the amendment, and (b) that the amendment, having been rejected by both Houses of the legislatures of 26 States and having been ratified only in five States between 1924 and 1927, had failed of ratification within a reasonable period and thus no longer was viable. *Coleman* v. *Miller*, 307 U.S., at 435–36.[50] The Supreme Court of Kansas denied the writ. *Coleman* v. *Miller*, 146 Kan. 390 (1937). That court, relying on the precedent of the Civil War Amendments, held:

> It is generally agreed by lawyers, statesmen and publicists who have debated this question that a state legislature which has rejected an amendment proposed by Congress may later reconsider its action and give its approval, but that a ratification once given cannot be withdrawn. (At 400).
>
> . . . . .
>
> It would seem, then, that a state legislature which has rejected an amendment proposed by congress may later reconsider its action and give its approval. (Willoughby on the Constitution, sec. 329a.).
>
> In a release from the department of state under date of April 20, 1935, attached as an exhibit to plaintiff's petition in this case, giving the status of the child-labor amendment, it appears that in five states, Indiana, Minnesota, New Hampshire, Pennsylvania and Utah, after the proposed amendment had been rejected, each of the states later adopted a resolution of ratification. When these states rejected the amendment, was their power with reference to the proposed amendment exhausted? If so, the subsequent ratification would be void. Is it to be seriously argued that the secretary of state could not count these five states in making up the total number of states necessary to adopt the amendment?
>
> Thus it appears to be an historical fact that many states have rejected proposed amendments, and have later ratified them. (At 401).

From the foregoing and from historical precedents, it is also true that where a state has once ratified an amendment it has no power thereafter to withdraw such ratification. To hold otherwise would make article 5 of the federal constitution read that the amendment should be valid "when ratified by three fourths of the states, each adhering to its vote until three fourths of all the legislatures shall have voted to ratify."

It is clear, then, both on principle and authority, that a proposed amendment once rejected by the legislature of a state may by later action of the same legislature be ratified; and *that when a proposed amendment has once been ratified the power to act on the proposed amendment ceases to exist. (At 403)* [emphasis added].

The Supreme Court of the United States affirmed the decision of the Supreme Court of Kansas in an unusually complicated ruling. *See* note 4, *supra.*

The opinion of the Court, written by Chief Justice Hughes and on this issue actually joined by Justices Stone and Reed, and presumably joined by Justices Black, Roberts, Frankfurter, and Douglas,[51] recited the historic precedent established on the occasion of the adoption of the Fourteenth and Fifteenth Amendments and observed that this "decision by the political departments of the Government as to the validity of the adoption of the Fourteenth Amendment has been accepted." 307 U.S., at 450.

The question whether a State has the power to change its position with regard to the adoption of a constitutional amendment does not seem to have become a serious issue in connection with any of the later amendments submitted to the States.

The problem, however, did arise indirectly in connection with legislation designed to establish procedures for calling constitutional conventions. In that context the Senate committee reports conceded that under existing law a State could not rescind its ratification of a constitutional amendment but took the position that the law should be "changed."[52] The bills therefore provided in effect that a State could rescind its ratification of a proposed constitutional amendment until it had been validly adopted. Both bills passed the Senate but died in the House of Representatives.[53]

B. The Application of Madison's Principle

When the Supreme Court held in *Dillon* v. *Gloss, supra,* that Congress has implied power under Article V to set a time period for ratification of a proposed amendment, it was writing on what was virtually *tabula rasa.* Likewise, in approaching the question whether Congress may extend a limitation once set, we think that historical understanding, while informative, cannot be thought of as conclusive.

With regard to whether a State might rescind during an "extension" period, there is certainly a temptation to assume that the question may be approached in the same manner because, no extension ever having been contemplated, it follows that the question of rescission during such a period could not have been contemplated. Were we to take such an approach, we could perhaps be easily persuaded by the argument that "[t]he extension of time for ratification but not for rescission would be...grotesque...."[54]

That argument appears to be that failure to provide for rescission would permit an amendment to be ratified without the "contemporaneous consensus" required by the Constitution (presumably required by Article V as interpreted in *Dillon* v. *Gloss, supra*). This lack of a "contemporaneous consensus" would, under this view, perhaps be evidenced by several or many attempted rescissions by States that would give a reasonable man reason to think that no consensus existed.

That analysis confuses two issues that should, we think, be sharply differentiated in the consideration of H.J. Res. 638. First is the issue whether the period of 14 years proposed in H.J. Res. 638 is "reasonable" in view of the interpretation placed on Art. V in *Dillon* v. *Gloss* and with which we are in agreement. If 14 years or possibly a lesser period is, in the judgment of Congress, "reasonable," then the question of the power of States to rescind in the last seven years of the 14-year period is irrelevant. The second issue is, of course, whether the States may rescind a prior ratification during the extension period because the will of its people has in fact changed since initial ratification. This argument would appear to reduce to the proposition that a seven-year extension can be viewed as "reasonable" only if no substantial number of States actually attempt to rescind their ratifications during the extension period. Under this view, the power to rescind functions as a sort of escape valve permitting the States themselves to determine what is or what is not a "reasonable" period of time by acts of rescission.

We are unable to agree with that analysis. In our view, the lesson of history, including prior congressional interpretation of Art. V with regard to the Fourteenth Amendment, is that States may not rescind a ratification. And we think *Dillon* v. *Gloss* and *Coleman* v. *Miller* are equally dispositive in rejecting any possibility that States, rather than Congress, are to have the final say concerning whether an amendment has been ratified within a "reasonable" time.

In our view, the most persuasive argument that Art. V permits rescission during an extension period is predicated on a notion that State legislatures may have relied on the seven-year period established in H.J.

Res. 208 by assuming that they would be held to their ratification for a seven-year period and no longer. We have examined the certifications of ratification submitted to GSA by the 35 States having ratified the ERA and are unable to conclude that such reliance is indicated, at least on the face of those documents. More importantly, we think that such a concept of ''reliance'' is essentially no different, in kind, from the proposal before the New York Convention to ratify the Constitution on a *conditional* basis, an act that James Madison viewed as invalid. We say ''no different in kind'' because, from a purely analytical point of view, the only difference would be that Congress' act of setting a seven-year limit in H.J. Res. 208 or in H.J. Res. 638 would have to be viewed as equivalent to Congress' extending to the States a right to ratify an amendment conditionally. We think that the whole thrust of history is that Art. V, as interpreted, does not permit States to rescind or otherwise place conditions upon their ratifications. If we are correct in this view, we think it follows that such a power can be granted only by an amendment to Art. V itself.

V. The Political Question Doctrine

Although we think that the constitutional questions raised by H.J. Res. 638 should be addressed on their merits without reference to the likelihood that the courts will finally resolve any or all of them, we recognize that the difficulty of those questions coupled with the uncertainty we (and presumably others) entertain with regard to our resolution of them can give rise to congressional interest in this question.

Prior to the decision in *Coleman* v. *Miller,* the Court consistently entertained and resolved questions arising out of the amendment and ratification process.[55] In *Coleman* itself, we think that a majority[56] of the Court squarely held that the effect of prior rejection on ratification was a political question not justiciable in the courts and that the same majority took the same view of the effect of rescission on final ratification by three-fourths of the States. We see no reason why the Court would change its prior position on the political nature of these questions unless perhaps if this aspect of *Coleman* were premised on the understanding that the answers to these questions had been firmly settled by history and were not subject to reversal by a future Congress.

There was, however, no clear majority in *Coleman,* as pointed out by Justice Black in his concurring opinion, for the position that courts could never review the question of reasonableness. Thus, we are not at all certain that the question of the reasonableness of the seven-year extension might not be subjected to judicial review in an appropriate case, particularly were ratification by the requisite three-fourths of the States to be obtained toward the end of the 14-year period.

We think that decisions of the Supreme Court subsequent to *Coleman*,[57] as well as the cases cited in note 55, *supra*, indicate that the questions of the power of Congress to extend a ratification, the vote by which such an extension must be adopted, and perhaps whether Congress might confer on the States a right to rescind[58] are more likely to be viewed as justiciable controversies in appropriate cases. We take this view because these questions do not appear to present situations in which there is either a textually demonstrable commitment of their resolution to the Congress or there are no judicially discoverable standards by which to resolve the questions presented.

Notes

35. We do not think anyone could seriously doubt that a State's rescission of its ratification subsequent to adoption of an amendment would be a meaningless act.

36. V Papers of Alexander Hamilton 147, 177 (Syrett ed. 1961).

37. The full text of Madison's letter is as follows:

"From James Madison[1]

N. York Sunday Evening
[July 20, 1788][2]

"My dear Sir

"Yours of yesterday is this instant come to hand & I have but a few minutes to answer it. I am sorry that your situation obliges you to listen to propositions of the nature you describe. My opinion is that a reservation of a right to withdraw if amendments be not decided on under the form of the Constitution within a certain time, is a conditional ratification, that it does not make N. York a member of the New Union, and consequently that[3] she could not be received on that plan. Compacts must be reciprocal, this principle would not in such a case be preserved. The Constitution requires an adoption *in toto* and *for ever*. It has been so adopted by the other States. An adoption for a limited time would be as defective as an adoption of some of the articles only. In short any *condition* whatever must viciate the ratification. What the new Congress by virtue of the power to admit new States, may be able disposed to do in such a case, I do not enquire as I suppose that is not the material point at present. I have not a moment to add more. Know my fervent wishes for your success & happiness.

Js. Madison

This idea of reserving right to withdraw was started at Richmd & considered as a conditional ratification which was itself considered as worse than a rejection: 1. In JCHW, I, 465, this letter is dated 'Sunday Evening.' After serving in the Virginia Ratifying Convention, Madison had resumed his seat in the Continental Congress. 2. This letter was written on the day after H wrote to Madison, July 19, 1788. 3. In MS, 'that that.' "

38. The Convention also defeated a motion reserving to the State of New York a right to withdraw from the Union after a certain number of years, unless the amendments proposed previously were submitted to a general convention. II J. Elliot's Debates 412 (1854). It is not apparent whether Madison's letter was brought to the attention of the N.Y. Convention. Madison's letter, *supra,* however, indicates that the mails between New York, where Madison served on the Continental Congress, and Poughkeepsie, the seat of the New York Convention, took only a day. Hence, it is likely that Madison's letter of July 20 was utilized during the crucial debates in the New York Convention on July 23, 1788.

39. *See* Ames, *Amendments to the Constitution of the United States, reprinted in* H. Doc. 353, 54th Cong., 2d Sess. (pt. 2) 300 n. 4 and 320 (1891).

40. Jameson, note 22 *supra,* at 630.

41. *Id.,* quoting Acts General Assembly, Ky., 1865, p. 157.

42. This figure is based on the recitals of the Proclamation of July 28, 1968, 15 Stat. 708. According to the Brief of the United States as *amicus curiae* in *Coleman* v. *Miller, supra* at 14, the Amendment had been rejected prior to ratification by seven States: Alabama, Arkansas, Florida, Georgia, Louisiana, North Carolina, and South Carolina, which, with the exception of Georgia, had ratified it prior to July 20, 1868.

43. The submission by Congress of a constitutional amendment to the States need not be presented to the President *(Hollingsworth* v. *Virginia, supra[)]*. It therefore would appear that a congressional determination as to whether an amendment has been adopted by the requisite number of States can be passed as a concurrent resolution which is not presented to the President. *See also* note 24 *supra.*

44. *See* Note, 49 Ind. L. J. 147, 151 (1973).

45. On April 11, 1870, the House adopted a resolution authorizing the celebration of the adoption of the Amendment in the Hall of the House of Representatives. 90 Cong. Globe 2586–2587 (1870).

46. In *Hawke* v. *Smith,* 253 U.S. 221 (1920), the Supreme Court reached the same result but for other reasons.

47. 65 Cong. Rec. 4493 (1924[)]. *See also id.,* at 2152–53.

48. This statement was based in part on *Dillon* v. *Gloss,* 256 U.S. 368 (1921).

49. *See Coleman* v. *Miller,* 307 U.S., at 473 (*Chronology of Child Labor Amendment,* footnote to dissenting opinion of Butler, J.), and the *amicus curiae* brief filed by the United States in *Coleman* v. *Miller,* note 34 *supra,* Appendices A and B.

50. The Child Labor Amendment, as noted *supra,* had no provision requiring its adoption within a specific period of time. This proposed amendment was never actually ratified by three-fourths of the States.

51. On this particular point, we think that the opinion of Chief Justice Hughes must rightly be thought of as an opinion of the Court as it is described at its outset. We say this because Justice Black and those joining his concurring opinion clearly reached the merits of the issues raised, 307 U.S., at 456 (under "compulsion" of the court's holding on the standing question) and also indicated that his disagreement with Hughes' opinion was limited to aspects of Hughes' opinion not relevant to the present discussion, *id.,* at 458.

52. The question of whether a State may rescind an application once made has not been decided by any precedent, nor is there any authority on the question. It is one for Congress to answer, Congress previously has taken the position that having once ratified an amendment, a State may not rescind.

The committee is of the view that the former ratification rule should not control this question and, further, should be changed with respect to ratifications. Since a two-thirds concensus among the States in a given period of time is necessary to call a convention, obviously the fact that a State has changed its mind is pertinent. An application is not a final action. A State is always free, of course, to reject a proposed amendment. Of course, once the constitutional requirement of petitions from two-thirds of the States has been met and the amendment machinery is set in motion, these considerations no longer hold, and rescission is no longer possible. On the basis of the same reasoning, a State should be permitted to retract its ratification, or to ratify a proposed amendment it previously rejected. Of course, once the amendment is a part of the Constitution, this power does not exist.

S. Rep. No. 336, 92d Cong. 1st Sess. 14 (1971); S. Rep. No. 293, 93d Cong., 1st Sess. 14 (1973).

53. The latest congressional recognition of the rule that a state cannot rescind its ratification of a constitutional amendment of which we are aware is Senator Bayh's statement on the floor of the Senate, delivered on March 6, 1974:

Mr. BAYH. Mr. President, one of the questions which has aroused considerable interest with respect to the proposed 27th amendment to the Constitution has been whether a State once it has ratified the amendment may later change its mind and rescind its ratification. The issue was first raised by the State of Nebraska which has now rescinded its earlier ratification. Several other states, in addition, have similar rescission resolutions pending before their State legislatures.

I am firmly convinced that, once a State legislature has exercised the powers given it by article V of the Congress, it has exhausted its powers in this regard and may not later go back and change its mind.

120 Cong. Rec. 5574 (1974).

54. Statement of Charles L. Black, Jr., Sterling Professor of Law, Yale University, on Extension of Time for Action on Amendments for the States, October 12, 1977.

55. *See Hollingsworth* v. *Virginia, supra; Dillon* v. *Gloss, supra, Hawke* v. *Smith, supra; The National Prohibition Cases, supra; Leser* v. *Garnett, supra; United States* v. *Sprague, supra.*

56. *See* note 51, *supra.*

57. *E.g., Baker* v. *Carr,* 369 U.S. 186 (1962); *Powell* v. *McCormack,* 395 U.S. 486 (1969).

58. Even assuming that the question of the effect of a rescission is non-justiciable under *Coleman,* as we do, it is possible that the Court would take a different approach were H.J. Res. 638 to be amended to provide explicitly for such a right to rescind. This is so because the power of Congress to grant such a right to the States by statute would perhaps be placed on a different footing.

2. Opinion of Counsel, Senate Subcommittee on Constitutional Amendments of the Committee on the Judiciary

On 20 February 1973, J. William Heckman, counsel for the U.S. Senate Committee on the Judiciary, Subcommittee on Constitutional Amendments, issued an opinion on rescission which was subsequently sent to Nebraska. The following excerpts are from that opinion.

[T]he purpose of this letter is to express our views on the question of whether a state may rescind its ratification of a Constitutional Amendment. Briefly the judicial opinions and, more importantly, the precedents established by the Congress itself make it clear that once a state has ratified an amendment, it has exhausted the only power conferred on it by Article V of the Constitution, and may not, therefore, validly rescind such action. . . .

When an amendment is proposed either by the Congress or by a Constitutional convention called by the Congress on the application of two thirds of the States and such an amendment is submitted to the legislatures of the states for ratification, the legislature is not exercising a legislative function, just as Congress, when it purposes, is not legislating [footnote deleted]. The legislature in ratifying is exercising a ministerial or constituent function; the ratifying process is equivalent to a roll call of the states. The Constitution empowers states to ratify only, since the object was to determine what the people want to add to their Constitution, not to take a poll concerning views on the subject of the amendment.

The question with which we are presently concerned is whether a legislature may change its action with respect to an amendment. It is one which has several times come up in practice. One view is that the first action by the legislature of a particular state is conclusive and binds future legislatures, whether the legislature rejects or ratifies. This position, which has received little support, was taken by the Supreme Court of Kentucky in *Wise v Chandler*, 270 Ky. 1, 108 S.W.end. (1937).

Heckman discussed the decision of the Kentucky Supreme Court in *Wise* v. *Chandler* and the contrary opinion of the Kansas Supreme Court in *Coleman* v. *Miller*. He concluded that the view of the Kansas court is supported by the commentators.

Judge Jameson in his treatise *On Constitutional Conventions: Their History, Powers, and Modes of Proceeding* [footnote deleted] concludes:

The language of the Constitution is, that amendments proposed by Congress, in the mode prescribed, 'shall be valid to all intents and purposes, as part of this Constitution, *when ratified by the legislatures of three-fourths of the several states.*' By this language is conferred upon the States, by the national Constitution, a special power; it is not a power belonging to them originally by virtue of rights reserved or otherwise. When exercised, as contemplated by the Constitution, by ratifying, it ceases to be a power, and any attempt to exercise it again must be nullity. But, until so exercised, the power undoubtedly, for a reasonable time at least, remains. . . . When ratified all power is expended. Until ratified the right to ratify remains. Jameson at p. 628 (emphasis in original)

The question was presented to the Supreme Court of the United States on writ of certiorari to the Kansas Supreme Court in the *Coleman* case. *(Coleman v. Miller,* 307 U.S. 433 (1939)). The Court held that the question of the effect to be given to reversals of action as to ratification by state legislatures was a "political" one to be decided by the Congress under its powers to implement Article V.

After quoting the U.S. Supreme Court in *Coleman* v. *Miller*, Heckman traced the history of congressional expression concerning the Fourteenth and Fifteenth amendments, during which Congress ignored attempted rescissions by several states.

Congress, therefore, has expressed itself quite definitively on this question. It is my legal opinion as Counsel of the Subcommittee on Constitutional Amendments of the United States Senate that once a State has exercised its only power under Article V of the United States Constitution and ratified an Amendment thereto, it has exhausted such power, and that any attempt subsequently to rescind such ratification is null and void. The Attorney General of the State of Idaho has recently expressed the same view in an opinion to the legislature of that state. A copy of his opinion is attached for your information.

Appendix C

Congressional Action

1. Adoption of the Fourteenth Amendment

a. EXCERPT FROM THE MESSAGE TO CONGRESS BY SECRETARY OF STATE WILLIAM H. SEWARD, DATED 20 JULY 1868, SETTING FORTH THE CIRCUMSTANCES SURROUNDING RATIFICATION OF THE FOURTEENTH AMENDMENT (15 STAT. 706–10).

And whereas by the second section of the act of Congress, approved the twentieth of April, one thousand eight hundred and eighteen, entitled "An act to provide for the publication of the laws of the United States, and for other purposes," it is made the duty of the Secretary of State forthwith to cause any amendment to the Constitution of the United States, which has been adopted according to the provisions of the said Constitution, to be published in the newspapers authorized to promulgate the laws, with his certificate specifying the States by which the same may have been adopted, and that the same has become valid, to all intents and purposes, as a part of the Constitution of the United States;

And whereas neither the act just quoted from, nor any other law, expressly or by conclusive implication, authorizes the Secretary of State to determine and decide doubtful questions as to the authenticity of the organization of State legislatures, or as to the power of any State legislature to recall a previous act or resolution of ratification of any amendment proposed to the Constitution;

And whereas it appears from official documents on file in this Department that the amendment to the Constitution of the United States, proposed as aforesaid, has been ratified by the legislatures of the States of Connecticut, New Hampshire, Tennessee, New Jersey, Oregon, Vermont, New York, Ohio, Illinois, West Virginia, Kansas, Maine, Nevada, Missouri, Indiana, Minnesota, Rhode Island, Wisconsin, Pennsylvania, Michigan, Massachusetts, Nebraska, and Iowa;

And whereas it further appears from documents on file in this Department that the amendment to the Constitution of the United States, proposed as aforesaid, has also been ratified by newly constituted and newly established bodies avowing themselves to be and acting as the legislatures, respectively, of the States of Arkansas, Florida, North Carolina, Louisiana, South Carolina, and Alabama;

And whereas it further appears from official documents on file in this Department that the legislatures of two of the States first above enumerated, to wit, Ohio and New Jersey, have since passed resolutions respectively withdrawing the consent of each of said States to the aforesaid amendment; and whereas it is deemed a matter of doubt and uncertainty whether such resolutions are not irregular, invalid, and therefore ineffectual for withdrawing the consent of the said two States, or of either of them, to the aforesaid amendment;

And whereas the whole number of States in the United States is thirty-seven, to wit: New Hampshire, Massachusetts, Rhode Island, Connecticut, New York, New Jersey, Pennsylvania, Delaware, Maryland, Virginia, North Carolina, South Carolina, Georgia, Vermont, Kentucky, Tennessee, Ohio, Louisiana, Indiana, Mississippi, Illinois, Alabama, Maine, Missouri, Arkansas, Michigan, Florida, Texas, Iowa, Wisconsin, Minnesota, California, Oregon, Kansas, West Virginia, Nevada, and Nebraska;

And whereas the twenty-three States first hereinbefore named, whose legislatures have ratified the said proposed amendment, and the six States next thereafter named, as having ratified the said proposed amendment by newly constituted and established legislative bodies, together constitute three fourths of the whole number of States in the United States:

Now, therefore, be it known that I, WILLIAM H. SEWARD, Secretary of State of the United States, by virtue and in pursuance of the second section of the act of Congress, approved the twentieth of April, eighteen hundred and eighteen, hereinbefore cited, do hereby certify that if the resolutions of the legislatures of Ohio and New Jersey ratifying the aforesaid amendment are to be deemed as remaining of full force and effect, notwithstanding the subsequent resolutions of the legislatures of those States, which purport to withdraw the consent of said States from such ratification, then the aforesaid amendment has been ratified in the manner hereinbefore mentioned, and so has become valid, to all intents and purposes, as a part of the Constitution of the United States.

b. EXCERPT FROM THE DEBATE IN THE SENATE
(CONGRESSIONAL GLOBE, 21 JULY 1868, p. 4266).

Mr. SHERMAN. I move that the Senate proceed to consider a resolution which I think will take but a moment, Senate resolution No. 166—declaring the ratification of the fourteenth article of amendment of the Constitution of the United States. It is lying upon the table.

Mr. MORTON. I hope the Senator from Ohio will waive that for a moment to allow me to call up the bridge bill.

Mr. SHERMAN. This resolution ought to be considered now. It will take no time, I think.

The PRESIDENT *pro tempore.* Is there any objection to taking up the resolution mentioned by the Senator from Ohio? . . .

. . .If there be no objection, the resolution will be considered as before the Senate.

Mr. SHERMAN. I will change the form of the resolution, and make it a concurrent resolution.

The Chief Clerk read the resolution, as follows:

Whereas the Legislatures of the States of Connecticut, Tennessee, New Jersey, Oregon, Vermont, West Virginia, Kansas, Missouri, Indiana, Ohio, Illinois, Minnesota, New York, Wisconsin, Pennsylvania, Rhode Island, Michigan, Nevada, New Hampshire, Massachusetts, Nebraska, Maine, Iowa, Arkansas, Florida, North Carolina, Alabama, South Carolina, and Louisiana, being three fourths and more of the several States of the Union, have ratified the fourteenth article of amendment to the Constitution of the United States duly proposed by two thirds of each House of the Thirty-Ninth Congress: Therefore,

Be it resolved by the Senate, (the House of Representatives concurring,) That said fourteenth article is hereby declared to be a part of the Constitution of the United States, and it shall be duly promulgated as such by the Secretary of State.

The resolution was adopted.

c. EXCERPT FROM THE DEBATE IN THE HOUSE
OF REPRESENTATIVES *(CONGRESSIONAL GLOBE,*
21 JULY 1868, pp. 4295–96).

Mr. BOUTWELL. I move to take up the concurrent resolution just received from the Senate.

There was no objection.

The Clerk read the concurrent resolution as follows:

IN SENATE OF THE UNITED STATES,
July 21, 1868

Whereas the Legislatures of the States of Connecticut, Tennessee, New Jersey, Oregon, Vermont, West Virginia, Kansas, Missouri, Indiana, Ohio, Illinois, Minnesota, New York, Wisconsin, Pennsylvania, Rhode Island, Michigan, Nevada, New Hampshire, Massachusetts, Nebraska, Maine, Iowa, Arkansas, Florida, North Carolina, and Louisiana, being three fourths and more of the several States of the Union, have ratified the fourteenth article of amendment to the Constitution of the United States, duly proposed by two thirds of each House of the Thirty-Ninth Congress; Therefore,

Resolved by the Senate, (the House of Representatives concurring.) That said fourteenth article is hereby declared to be a part of the Constitution of the United States, and it shall be duly promulgated as such by the Secretary of State.

Attest: GEO. C. GORHAM, *Secretary.*

. . . . .

Mr. SCOFIELD. Is there any information in the possession of the House that Georgia has ratified that fourteenth article?

The SPEAKER. The Chair has a dispatch.

Mr. WASHBURNE, of Illinois. Let it be read.

Mr. BROOKS. I object unless we have read the withdrawal by Ohio and New Jersey of their assent to that amendment. . . .

Mr. BOUTWELL. I withdraw the call for the previous question, and ask the Clerk to read the dispatch which I send to the desk.

The Clerk read as follows:

ATLANTA, GEORGIA, *July* 21, 1868.

To SCHUYLER COLFAX.
Speaker House of Representatives:

Fourteenth article and fundamental conditions adopted by majority of thirty-four on joint ballot.

RUFUS D. BULLOCK,
Governor-elect.

Mr. MAYNARD. I hope the State of Alabama will be included in the resolution.

Mr. BOUTWELL. I move to amend the resolution by inserting "Georgia."

Mr. BROOKS. On a mere private telegram? How do you know that that came over the wires?

Mr. BROOMALL. We take it on faith.

The SPEAKER. The Chair doubts whether this is an official notice such as is required. It should be sent by mail.

Mr. BOUTWELL. I withdraw the motion to amend.

Mr. ELDRIDGE. I desire to propound a question to the gentleman from Massachusetts—whether this dispatch came into his hands through the post-mortem examination committee?

Mr. BOUTWELL. I have no knowledge of it.

Mr. ELDRIDGE. Or whether it was a captured telegram that came in a legitimate way of business?

Mr. BOUTWELL. I demand the previous question.

The previous question was seconded and the main question ordered.

Mr. HOLMAN and Mr. ELDRIDGE demanded the yeas and nays.

The yeas and nays were ordered.

Mr. HOLMAN. I believe the proposition is divisible. I call for a separate vote on the preamble.

The SPEAKER. It is divisible; a separate vote will be taken on the preamble. The question now is on agreeing to the resolution.

The question was taken; and it was decided in the affirmative—yeas 127, nays 33, not voting 55. . . .

So the resolution was agreed to.

The question recurred on agreeing to the preamble.

Mr. BOUTWELL. I demand the previous question.

The previous question was seconded and the main question ordered.

Mr. ELDRIDGE. I demand the yeas and nays.

The yeas and nays were ordered.

The question was taken; and it was decided in the affirmative—yeas 127, nays 35, not voting 53. . . .

d. EXCERPT FROM THE PROCLAMATION BY PRESIDENT ANDREW JOHNSON, DATED 27 JULY 1868 (15 STAT. 708).

WHEREAS, by an act of Congress entitled ''An act to admit the States of North Carolina, South Carolina, Louisiana, Georgia, Alabama, and Florida to representation in Congress,'' passed the twenty-fifth day of June, one thousand eight hundred and sixty-eight, it is declared that it is made the duty of the President within ten days after receiving official information of the ratification by the legislature of either of said States of a proposed amendment to the Constitution known as article fourteen, to issue a proclamation announcing that fact; and whereas a paper was received at the Department of State, this twenty-seventh day of July, one thousand eight hundred and sixty-eight, purporting to be a joint resolution of the Senate and House of Representatives of the General Assembly of the State of Georgia, ratifying the said proposed amendment, and also purporting to have passed the two said Houses respectively on the twenty-first of July, one thousand eight hundred and sixty-eight, and to have been approved by Rufus B. Bullock, who therein signs himself Governor of Georgia, which paper is also attested by the signatures of Benjamin Conley, as President of the Senate, and R. L. McWhorters, as Speaker of the House of Representatives, and is further attested by the signatures of A. E. Marshall, as Secretary of the Senate, and M. A. Hardin, as Clerk of the House of Representatives:

Now, therefore, be it known that I, ANDREW JOHNSON, President of the United States of America, in compliance with and execution of the act of Congress before mentioned, do issue this my proclamation announcing the fact of the ratification of the said amendment by the legislature of the State of Georgia in the manner hereinbefore set forth.

e. EXCERPTS FROM THE PROCLAMATION BY SECRETARY OF STATE WILLIAM H. SEWARD, DATED 28 JULY 1868 (15 STAT. 708).

WHEREAS by an act of Congress passed on the twentieth of April, one thousand eight hundred and eighteen, entitled, "An act to provide for the publication of the laws of the United States and for other purposes," it is declared that whenever official notice shall have been received at the Department of State that any amendment which heretofore has been and hereafter may be proposed to the Constitution of the United States has been adopted according to the provisions of the Constitution, it shall be the duty of the said Secretary of State forthwith to cause the said amendment to be published in the newspapers authorized to promulgate the laws, with his certificate, specifying the States by which the same may have been adopted, and that the same has become valid to all intents and purposes as a part of the Constitution of the United States.

And whereas the Congress of the United States, on or about the sixteenth day of June, one thousand eight hundred and sixty-six, submitted to the legislatures of the several States a proposed amendment to the Constitution in the following words, to wit:

[Quoting Fourteenth Amendment]

And whereas the Senate and House of Representatives of the Congress of the United States, on the twenty-first day of July, one thousand eight hundred and sixty-eight, adopted and transmitted to the Department of State a concurrent resolution, which concurrent resolution is in the words and figures following, to wit:—

"IN SENATE OF THE UNITED STATES,
"July 21, 1868.

"Whereas the legislatures of the States of Connecticut, Tennessee, New Jersey, Oregon, Vermont, West Virginia, Kansas, Missouri, Indiana, Ohio, Illinois, Minnesota, New York, Wisconsin, Pennsylvania, Rhode Island, Michigan, Nevada, New Hampshire, Massachusetts, Nebraska, Maine, Iowa, Arkansas, Florida, North Carolina, Alabama, South Carolina, and Louisiana, being three fourths and more of the several States of the Union, have ratified the fourteenth article of amendment to the Constitution of the United States, duly proposed by two thirds of each House of the Thirty-ninth Congress; therefore,

"Resolved by the Senate (the House of Representatives concurring,) That said fourteenth article is hereby declared to be a part of the Constitution of the United States, and it shall be duly promulgated as such by the Secretary of State.

"Attest: GEO. C. GORHAM, *Secretary.*

"IN THE HOUSE OF REPRESENTATIVES,
July 21, 1868.

"Resolved, That the House of Representatives concur in the foregoing concurrent resolution of the Senate 'declaring the ratification of the fourteenth article of amendment of the Constitution of the United States.'

"Attest: EDWD. McPHERSON, *Clerk."*

And whereas official notice has been received at the Department of State that the legislatures of the several States next hereinafter named have, at the times respectively herein mentioned, taken the proceedings hereinafter recited upon or in relation to the ratification of the said proposed amendment, called article fourteenth, namely:

The legislature of Connecticut ratified the amendment June 30th, 1866; the legislature of New Hampshire ratified it July 7th, 1866; the legislature of Tennessee ratified it July 19th, 1866; the legislature of New Jersey ratified it September 11th, 1866, and the legislature of the same State passed a resolution in April, 1868, to withdraw its consent to it; the legislature of Oregon ratified it September 19th, 1866; the legislature of Texas rejected it November 1st, 1866; the legislature of Vermont ratified it on or previous to November 9th, 1866; the legislature of Georgia rejected it November 13th, 1866, and the legislature of the same State ratified it July 21st, 1868; the legislature of North Carolina rejected it December 4th, 1866, and the legislature of the same State ratified it July 4th, 1868; the legislature of South Carolina rejected it December 20th, 1866, and the legislature of the same State ratified it July 9th, 1868; the legislature of Virginia rejected it January 9th, 1867; the legislature of Kentucky rejected it January 10th, 1867; the legislature of New York ratified it January 10th, 1867; the legislature of Ohio ratified it January 11th, 1867, and the legislature of the same State passed a resolution in January, 1868, to withdraw its consent to it; the legislature of Illinois ratified it January 15th, 1867; the legislature of West Virginia ratified it January 16th, 1867; the legislature of Kansas ratified it January 18th, 1867; the legislature of Maine ratified it January 19th, 1867; the legislature of Nevada ratified it January 22d, 1867; the legislature of Missouri ratified it on or previous to January 26th, 1867; the legislature of Indiana ratified it January 29th, 1867; the legislature of Minnesota ratified it February 1st, 1867; the legislature of Rhode Island ratified it February 7th, 1867; the legislature of Delaware rejected it February 7th, 1867; the legislature of Wisconsin ratified it February 13th, 1867; the legislature of Pennsylvania ratified it February 13th, 1867; the legislature of Michigan ratified it February 15th, 1867; the legislature of Massachusetts ratified it March 20th, 1867; the legislature of Maryland rejected it March 23d, 1867; the legislature of Nebraska ratified it June 15th, 1867; the legislature of Iowa ratified it April 3d, 1868; the legislature of Arkansas ratified it April 6th, 1868; the legislature of Florida ratified it June 9th, 1868; the legislature of Louisiana ratified it July 9th, 1868; and the legislature of Alabama ratified it July 13th, 1868.

Now, therefore, be it known that I, WILLIAM H. SEWARD, Secretary of State of the United States, in execution of the aforesaid act, and of the aforesaid concurrent resolution of the 21st of July, 1868, and in conformance thereto, do hereby direct the said proposed amendment to the Constitution of the United States to be published in the newspapers authorized to promulgate the laws of the United States, and I do hereby certify that the said proposed amendment has been adopted in the manner hereinbefore mentioned by the States specified in the said concurrent resolution, namely the States of Connecticut, New Hampshire, Tennessee, New Jersey, Oregon, Vermont, New York, Ohio, Illinois, West Virginia, Kansas, Maine, Nevada, Missouri, Indiana, Minnesota, Rhode Island, Wisconsin, Pennsylvania, Michigan, Massachusetts, Nebraska, Iowa, Arkansas, Florida, North Carolina, Louisiana, South Carolina, Alabama, and also by the legislature of the State of Georgia; the States thus specified being more than three fourths of the States of the United States.

And I do further certify that the said amendment has become valid to all intents and purposes as a part of the Constitution of the United States.

2. Adoption of the Fifteenth Amendment

a. EXCERPT FROM THE PROCLAMATION BY SECRETARY OF STATE HAMILTON FISH, DATED 30 MARCH 1870 (16 STAT. 1131–32).

[Quoting Fifteenth Amendment]

And, further, that it appears from official documents on file in this Department that the amendment to the Constitution of the United States, proposed as aforesaid, has been ratified by the legislatures of the States of North Carolina, West Virginia, Massachusetts, Wisconsin, Maine, Louisiana, Michigan, South Carolina, Pennsylvania, Arkansas, Connecticut, Florida, Illinois, Indiana, New York, New Hampshire, Nevada, Vermont, Virginia, Alabama, Missouri, Mississippi, Ohio, Iowa, Kansas, Minnesota, Rhode Island, Nebraska, and Texas, in all twenty nine States.

And, further, that the States whose legislatures have so ratified the said proposed amendment constitute three fourths of the whole number of States in the United States.

And further, that it appears from an official document on file in this Department that the legislature of the State of New York has since passed resolutions claiming to withdraw the said ratification of the said amendment which had been made by the legislature of that State, and of which official notice had been filed in this Department.

And, further, that it appears from an official document on file in this Department that the legislature of Georgia has by resolution ratified the said proposed amendment:

Now, therefore, be it known that I, HAMILTON FISH, Secretary of State of the United States, by virtue and in pursuance of the second section of the act of Congress approved the twentieth day of April, in the year eighteen hundred and eighteen, entitled ''An act to provide for the publication of the laws of the United States and for other purposes,'' do hereby certify that the amendment aforesaid has become valid to all intents and purposes as part of the Constitution of the United States.

3. Reaction to *Hawke* v. *Smith* (1920)

a. EXCERPTS FROM THE DEBATE IN THE SENATE OVER THE PROPOSAL BY SENATOR JAMES W. WADSWORTH OF NEW YORK TO AMEND ARTICLE V OF THE CONSTITUTION, 19 MARCH 1924 (65 *CONGRESSIONAL RECORD* 4493).

[This bill never came to a vote.]

"Article —.

"The Congress, whenever two-thirds of both houses shall deem it necessary, shall propose amendments to this Constitution, or, upon the application of two-thirds of the legislatures of the several States, shall call a convention for proposing amendments, which, in either case, shall be valid to all intents and purposes as a part of this Constitution when ratified by a vote of the qualified electors in three-fourths of the several States, said election to be held under such rules and regulations as each State shall prescribe and that until three-fourths of the States shall have ratified, or more than one-fourth of the States shall have rejected, a proposed amendment any State may in like manner change its vote: *Provided,* That if at any time more than one-fourth of the States have rejected the proposed amendment, said rejection shall be final and further consideration thereof by the States shall cease: *Provided further,* That any amendment proposed hereunder shall be inoperative unless it shall have been ratified as an amendment to the Constitution as provided in the Consitution within six years from the date of submission hereof to the States by the Congress: *Provided further,* That no State, without its consent, shall be deprived of its equal suffrage in the Senate."

Mr. WADSWORTH. Mr. President, on December 6, 1923, this joint resolution was introduced. In its original form it is, I think, an exact duplicate of the joint resolution introduced in the last Congress, and it had a great deal of consideration from the Committee on the Judiciary, including a hearing. It would be well worth the time of Senators who are interested in the preservation of the integrity of the Federal Constitution to get a copy of that hearing and read it. No hearing was held this year; but the committee, as I happen to know, has had many discussions on the subject, first in the subcommittee and then in the full committee.

In my remarks up to this point I have endeavored to point out three principal defects in the present machinery for the consideration of Federal amendments:

First, the people can have no participation in it, as the result of the Ohio case.

Second, hold-over legislatures, composed of members who were elected long before the submission of an amendment, may ratify, and have done so, even in spite of their State constitutions. That should be corrected.

Third, there is grave doubt whether any State can change its vote from the affirmative to the negative. That certainly should be corrected.

The amendment as originally introduced sought only to meet those three objections, and sought to do it in such fashion as to make just as little change as possible in Article V. Some very well trained minds gave their attention to this matter long, long before I ever saw it in bill form; and it was not until after weeks and weeks of discussion, held privately, that a group of people finally arrived at the language which can be found in the original joint resolution on page 2, commencing with line 6.

The joint resolution as originally introduced makes no change in the manner of the submission of an amendment. The Congress may submit the amendments either to conventions called in the States or to the legislatures, but it goes on and provides that the members of at least one house in each of the legislatures which may ratify shall be elected after such amendments have been proposed. . . .

Mr. WADSWORTH. It is apparent that under Article V, as now drawn, no State can change its vote from the affirmative to the negative in the matter of a constitutional amendment. Once ratified by a State, that State can not change, even though it does so before a sufficient number of States have ratified so as to insert the amendment in the Constituion itself. Tennessee tried to change. It can not be done under Article V.

Mr. WALSH of Massachusetts. Mr. President, having once rejected, can it change?

Mr. WADSWORTH. Yes; the legislature of a State may change from the negative to the affirmative at any time, and there is now pending before the States of the Union a proposed amendment to the Federal Constitution submitted away back about 1820.

Mr. ASHURST. Mr. President, will the Senator yield at that point?

Mr. WADSWORTH. I yield.

Mr. ASHURST. If I understood the Senator correctly, he said that a State having voted affirmatively on the ratification of an amendment can not change its vote.

Mr. WADSWORTH. It can not.

Mr. ASHURST. I appreciate the study which the able Senator has given this amendment, but I do not agree with that conclusion. Does the Senator use the Tennessee case as a precedent?

Mr. WADSWORTH. In part.

Mr. ASHURST. I do not think it entirely fair to inject my personal opinion into the matter, but I disagree with the Senator's conclusion on that point. I assert that a State, no matter how it may have voted, has the right to change its vote, provided it changes it before other States have acted in sufficient number to cause a ratification; but it is immaterial. I do not want to interrupt the Senator's fine argument, but I simply did not want to be committed to that proposition.

Mr. WADSWORTH. I may have stated the matter too emphatically.

Mr. ASHURST. But the Senator is entirely correct; the Senator is historically correct when he says that when an amendment is once submitted by the Congress there is no power known to withdraw it from the consideration of the States. They have forever to ratify it.

Mr. WADSWORTH. It is there forever. There is one there now.

Mr. ASHURST. Yes, sir.

Mr. McKELLAR. I think that is what the Supreme Court held.

Mr. WADSWORTH. Am I right when I say that the amendment which is now pending has something to do with forbidding American citizens to accept titles of nobility?

Mr. ASHURST. Yes. The able Senator stated that some amendments were pending for many years. There were two submitted on the 15th of September, 1789, and they are still pending, according to the last returns.

Mr. WADSWORTH. They are there all right. They can be taken up and ratified now.

Mr. ASHURST. Exactly. Another one, to which the learned Senator has referred, was submitted in 1810.

Mr. WADSWORTH. That is the one I had in mind.

Mr. ASHURST. That proposed amendment prohibited citizens of the United States from accepting gifts, bounties, or perquisites from a foreign country. It has been pending for 110 years and has not been ratified, according to the latest returns. Another one is still pending; and I think the able Senator will do a great public service, in addition to the great public services he has already rendered, if he will hammer away not only upon the necessity of giving the people some chance to say what they think about the form of government they are living under in the way of expressing their approval of constitutional amendments, but upon the necessity of limiting the time within which a State may act.

I thank the Senator. I shall not interrupt him again.

Mr. WADSWORTH. I may have been overemphatic or too sure of my ground when I said a moment ago that a State can not change from the affirmative to the negative. It may be that it can.

Mr. ASHURST. Let me say to the Senator that on that point there is a very sharp division of opinion amongst lawyers.

Mr. WADSWORTH. Yes; there is.

Mr. ASHURST. I adhere to the opinion that a State, if its action is not conclusive or determinative, may change.

b. EXCERPT FROM THE DEBATE IN THE HOUSE OF REPRESENTATIVES OVER THE PROPOSAL TO AMEND ARTICLE V, 20 JANUARY 1925 (66 *CONGRESSIONAL RECORD* 2159).

[Finis J. Garrett of Tennessee:] A State which has said "no" may now change and say "yes." What can be the injustice in permitting a corollary whereby it may, within reasonable time limits, change from "yes" to "no"?

The question of the right of a State to reconsider its action upon amendment has been the subject of much profound discussion. It has never been specifically passed upon by the Supreme Court. In the case of the fourteenth amendment three States—New Jersey, Ohio, and Oregon—after having ratified subsequently reconsidered and withdrew their consent. The two first did this before the proclamation of the Secretary of State issued July 18, and he issued a statement reciting the facts and declaring that it had been ratified provided these States were to be counted, notwithstanding their reconsideration. Congress immediately passed a concurrent resolution declaring the ratification valid and sufficient, and so on July 28 Secretary Seward, accepting the dictum of Congress, issued a second proclamation declaring it a part of the organic law. It is for this reason, among others, that many lawyers have taken the position that the fourteenth amendment was never legally ratified.

New York, in the case of the fifteenth amendment, ratified on April 14, 1869, but on January 5, 1870, passed resolutions withdrawing consent. This was before the Secretary of State had issued the proclamation, but New York was nevertheless included therein as one of the ratifying States. There were three-fourths without New York, however, and so her action was of no legal moment.

On the other hand, there are several instances where States reconsidered acts of rejection of the thirteenth, fourteenth, and fifteenth amendments and ratified, and concerning these actions reconsidering negation no question apparently was ever made by the Secretary of State, or, so far as I know, by the Congress.

In practice, therefore, it may be said—and I think it is generally regarded to be—the law that a State may reconsider and change a rejection, but may not reconsider and change a ratification.

Jameson, in his work on constitutional law, in reasoning upon the proposition says, in substance, that this is true because the amendment is submitted for consideration; that after ratification the legislature has lost control. It has passed from its forum, so to speak. But the act of rejection does not have a similar effect. It does not put it beyond their reach if they choose to reach again.

I believe and undertake to maintain that there is no more reason in governmental ethics why an affirmative act should not have the right of reconsideration than a negative prior to the time when the affirmative act actually makes law, and hence the third proposed change.

4. Ervin Bill on Constitutional Convention Procedures

The Subcommittee on Separation of Powers of the Committee on the Judiciary, chaired by Senator Sam Ervin of North Carolina, on 12 April 1973 had a bill before it (S.1272) to establish procedures for the calling of a federal constitutional convention by the states, pursuant to Article V. The following excerpt is from this bill (119 Congressional Record 8357).

RESCISSION OF RATIFICATIONS

SEC. 13. (a) Any State may rescind its ratification of a proposed amendment by the same processes by which it ratified the proposed amendment, except that no State may rescind when there are existing valid ratifications of such amendment by three-fourths of the States.

(b) Any State may ratify a proposed amendment even though it previously may have rejected the same proposal.

(c) Questions concerning State ratification or rejection of amendments proposed to the Constitution of the United States, shall be determined solely by the Congress of the United States, and its decisions shall be binding on all others, including State and Federal courts.

a. EXCERPTS FROM SENATE REPORT NO. 93–293, 92d CONG., 1ST SESS. (1971), BY THE SUBCOMMITTEE ON SEPARATION OF POWERS (119 *CONGRESSIONAL RECORD* 22732–36).

Although the impetus for this legislation was initially provided by the public concern over accumulating petitions for a convention to consider an amendment regarding reapportionment, the committee has not considered the legislation in the narrow light of any single issue. The committee believes that the responsibility of Congress under the Constitution is to enact legislation which makes article V meaningful. . . .

Background of Article V

Because so much confusion has been disseminated about the origins of article V, it is not inappropriate to set forth here, in capsule form, the development in the Convention of 1787 of the provisions of article V. In the words of Philip B. Kurland:

However natural it may now seem for the Constitution to provide for its own amendment, we should remember Holmes's warning against confusing the familiar with the necessary. There are other, more recent, national constitutions that make no such provision. The nature of the political compromises that resulted from the 1787 Convention was reason enough for those present not to tolerate a ready method of undoing what they had done. Article V, like most of the important provisions of the Constitution, must be attributed more to the prevailing spirit of compromise that dominated the Convention than to dedication to principle.

Although the original Virginia plan provided for a method of amendment, the first essential question resolved by the Convention was whether any method of amendment should be provided. Despite strong opposition from men such as Charles Pinckney of South Carolina, the Convention soon agreed in principle to the desirability of specifying a mode for amendment, with Mason, Randolph, and Madison of Virginia, Gouverneur Morris of Pennsylvania, Elbridge Gerry of Massachusetts, and Hamilton of New York leading the Convention toward accepting the necessity of such a provision.

The Virginia plan not only specified an amendment process but provided also that the National Legislature be excluded from participation in that process. And it was on the question of the proper role of Congress that the second major conflict was fought. When first reported by the Committee of Detail, the provision called for amendment by a convention to be called— apparently as a ministerial action—by the National Legislature on application of the legislatures of two-thirds of the States. Although this plan was first approved, the issue was again raised on Gerry's motion for reconsideration, seconded by Hamilton, and supported by Madison. On reconsideration, Sherman of Connecticut sought to have the power given to the National Legislature to propose amendments to the States for their approval. Wilson of Pennsylvania suggested that the approval of two-thirds of the States should be sufficient, and when this proposal was lost he was able to secure consent to a requirement of three-fourths of the States. At this point Madison offered what was in effect a substitute for the Committee of Detail's amended recommendation. It read, as the final draft was to read, in terms of alternative methods. Two-thirds of each House of Congress or two-thirds of the State legislatures could propose amendments. The amendments were to be ratified when approved either by three-fourths of the State legislatures or by conventions in three-fourths of the States. This compromise eventually overcame the second difficulty. By providing for alternative methods of procedure, the Madison proposal also made possible the compromise between those who would, from fear of the reticence of the National Legislature to correct its own abuses, utilize the convention as the means of initiating change, and those who, like Mason, wanted the National Legislature to be the sole sponsor of amendments. . . .

Article V, which resulted from these deliberations, must be attributed largely to Madison, with obvious active participation of Hamilton . . . ("Article V and the Amending Process," by Philip B. Kurland, in 1, *An American Primer* 130–131 edited by Daniel J. Boorstin (1966)).

Although constitutional conventions, as used by the States, generally have been reserved for wholesale, as distinguished from piecemeal, constitutional revision, there is nothing in the record of the debates at the Philadelphia Convention which discloses any comparable intention on the part of the Framers. On the contrary, the latter refrained from any evaluation or differentiation of the two procedures for amendment incorporated into article V: they tended to view the convention merely as an alternative safeguard available to the States whenever Congress ceased to be responsive to popular will and persisted in a refusal to originate and submit constitutional amendments for ratification.

The history of the use of the amendments process also was stated briefly by Professor Kurland:

Although the Constitution has been the subject of 24* different amendments, resort has never once been made to a national convention to initiate the process. And only once, in the case of the 21st amendment, was the State-convention process utilized for purposes of ratifying an amendment.

*Now 26.

For the most part, the amendments have been minor rather than major rearrangements of the constitutional plan. The first 10 amendments, the Bill of Rights, came so hard on the heels of the original document that they must be treated, for almost all purposes, as part of it. The only truly basic changes came in the Civil War amendments, the 13th, 14th, and 15th. Although intended primarily for the benefit of the Negroes, who ultimately were the beneficiaries, the amendments have proved to be the essential vehicles for the transfer of power from the States to the National Government and, within the National Government, to the Supreme Court, which has since exercised a veto power over the actions of the State legislatures, executives, and judiciaries. . . .[T]here can be little doubt of the truth of Felix Frankfurter's observation that there has been throughout our history an "absence of any widespread or sustained demand for a general revision of the Constitution."

On the other hand, it should be noted that some of the amendments have been attributable solely to the need to correct a Supreme Court construction of the Constitution. Thus, the 11th amendment was promulgated to overrule the case of *Chisholm* v. *Georgia*, 2 Dall. 419 (1793), in which the Court held that a sovereign immunity was not available as a defense to suit by a citizen of one State against another State. The necessity for the Civil War amendments derived in no small measure from the awful case of *Dred Scott* v. *Stanford*. 19 How. 393 (1857). The 16th amendment, authorizing the income tax, was a direct consequence of the Court's highly dubious decisions in *Pollock* v. *Farmers' Loan and Trust Co.*, 157 U.S. 429 (1895), 158 U.S. 601 (1895).

The other major category of amendments includes those relating to the mechanics of the National Government itself. These are due, first, to the need to eliminate ambiguities that became apparent through experience and, second, to the tendency toward extension of the franchise, a movement notable in all democratic countries during the 19th and 20th centuries. In the first group fall the 12th amendment, made necessary by the tied vote for Jefferson and Burr in the 1800 election; the 20th amendment, a response to the increased effiency of communications and transportation that made it possible to provide for the succession of the newly elected government at a date much closer to the election, as well as to the need to eliminate the ambiguities about filling a presidential vacancy; the 22nd amendment, which adopted George Washington's notion that two terms were enough for any man to occupy the Presidency, an unwritten constitutional tradition broken by Franklin Delano Roosevelt's election to the office for four successive terms. In the second category, the amendments that enhance popular sovereignty, fall the 17th, providing for popular election of Senators; the 19th, providing for women's suffrage; the 23rd, giving a voice to citizens of the District of Columbia in the election of the President; and the 24th eliminating the poll tax as a requirement for voting in national elections.

The only two other amendments are concrete evidence of the undesirability of promulgating a minority's notions of morality as part of the Nation's fundamental law. The 18th amendment, the prohibition amendment, was a ban on commerce in intoxicating liquors. The horrible results of the ''noble experiment'' that led an entire nation into a lawlessness from which it has never recovered caused the repeal of the 18th amendment by the 21st amendment.

Perhaps the primary importance of article V may be found in the *in terrorem* effect of an ultimate appeal to the people for the correction of the abuses of their government. But it is not a weapon ready for use and its cumbersome method is both its virtue and its vice. (Kurland, *op. cit. supra*, at 132–134.)

Although the convention route has never been used as a means of proposing amendments, its usefulness has been demonstrated. The campaign for direct elections of Senators was stymied for decades by the understandable reluctance of the Senate to propose an amendment which jeopardized the tenure of many of its Members. Frustrated by the Senate, the reform movement shifted to the States, and a series of petitions seeking to invoke the convention process were submitted to Congress. Rather than risk its fate at the hands of a convention, the Senate then relented and approved the proposed amendment, which was speedily ratified. The history of the 17th amendment illustrates the usefulness of having a method by which a recalcitrant Congress can be bypassed when it stands in the way of the desires of the country for constitutional change. . . .

Authority of Congress to Specify Procedures for a Constitutional Convention Called by the States

It is the opinion of the committee that Congress unquestionably has the authority to legislate about the process of amendment by convention, and to settle every point not actually settled by article V of the Constitution itself. This is implicit in article V. Obviously the 50 State legislatures cannot themselves legislate on this subject. The constitutional convention cannot do so for it must first be brought into being. All this is left, therefore, to Congress, which in any event, in respect to other issues not specifically settled by the Constitution, has the residual power to legislate on matters that require uniform settlement.

Congress has full authority to prescribe and determine what a valid application shall be and is further authorized to provide as it chooses for the selection of delegates and the procedures that will govern the convention's operations. As to the first point, Congress is made the agency for calling the convention, and it is hard to see why Congress should have been brought into the matter at all unless it were expected to determine when sufficient appropriate applications had been received. As to the second point, the same argument is compelling; if Congress were not expected to provide for the selection and procedures of the convention, why were no provisions made for those matters in article V itself? It would have been perfectly simple for the article to have provided for delegation of those arrangements to the States. When we add to this argument the weight of the necessary and proper clause and the authority of *Coleman* v. *Miller* for the proposition that the amending process is in the congressional domain, the conclusion is inescapable. Congress has plenary power to provide for the selection and procedures of the convention. Nor is Congress hampered here by the provisions of article V relating to ratification. The States as States must give approval to proposed amendments, because that is what article V says. But the article says nothing at all about how the convention shall be chosen or operate; and, for the reasons given, that omission leaves decision on those matters in the hands of Congress.

As Mr. Theodore Sorensen said in his testimony before the sub-committee:

The constitutional authority of Congress to establish rules and procedures regularizing the use or application of principles set forth in the Constitution has been too frequently exercised to be doubted today. Moreover, because State legislatures in proposing amendments via the convention route for performing a Federal function derived from the Federal Constitution, they could not be heard in court to complain about the imposition of reasonable standards and procedures by the Federal Congress, so long as their fundamental right to amend the Constitution is not thereby impaired. . . .

In short, I fully concur with Chairman Ervin that Congress has both the power and the duty to implement article V, to prevent the crisis and chaos that would otherwise result and to restrict any such convention to those topics that are specified in the applications of State legislatures. . . .

Time within Which the Application for Constitutional Conventions Must Be Filed

Article V is silent on the question of how long a proposed amendment should remain available for ratification or rejection by the States. It is likewise silent on the question of how long applications for a convention should remain valid. There is general agreement that, to be meaningful, applications for a constitutional convention to propose an amendment on a single subject should be a contemporaneous recognition by the States of the need for solution of a constitutional problem. There is some difference of opinion about the time period that is an appropriate measure of this contemporaneity. In the recent past, in making provision for the ratification of amendments proposed by Congress, 7 years has been specified as the appropriate time period within which ratification should take place. The bill provides that the same period—7 years—shall be the valid period. A shorter time, for instance 1 or 2 years, would not afford the States adequate time for debate and deliberation on so fundamental a question as a proposed constitutional amendment. On the other hand, a much longer time, say 15 years, would not satisfy the reasoned desire for consensus. . . .

Rescission of Applications and Ratifications

The question of whether a State may rescind an application once made has not been decided by any precedent, nor is there any authority on the question. It is one for Congress to answer. Congress previously has taken the position that having once ratified an amendment, a State may not rescind.

The committee is of the view that the former ratification rule should not control this question and, further, should be changed with respect to ratifications. Since a two-thirds consensus among the States in a given period of time is necessary to call a convention, obviously the fact that a State has changed its mind is pertinent. An application is not a final action. A State is always free, of course, to reject a proposed amendment. On these grounds, it is best to provide for rescission. Of course, once the constitutional requirement of petitions from two-thirds of the States has been met and the amendment machinery is set in motion, these considerations no longer hold, and rescission is no longer possible. On the basis of the same reasoning, a State should be permitted to retract its ratification, or to ratify a proposed amendment it previously rejected. Of course, once the amendment is a part of the Constitution, this power does not exist.

b. EXCERPT FROM THE DEBATE IN THE SENATE, 19 OCTOBER 1971 (117 *CONGRESSIONAL RECORD* 36754).

STATE APPLICATIONS CALLING FOR CONVENTION TO PROPOSE CONSTI-
TUTIONAL AMENDMENTS FROM 1787 TO SEPTEMBER 1971 BY SUBJECT
MATTER

Dates	Subject matter of amendment proposed	Number of States submitting applications on subject
1788 to 1929	General revision of Constitution	22
1833	Against protective tariff	1
1893 to 1911	Direct election of Senators	31
1906 to 1916	Prohibition of polygamy	27
1911	Control of trusts	1
1913	Constitutionality of State enactments	1
1920	Popular ratification of amendments	1
1925 to 1932	Repeal of 18th amendment	5
1927 and 1935	Taxation of Federal and State securities	2
1935	Federal regulation of wages and hours of labor	1
1939	The Townsend Plan	1
1939 to 1960	Limitation of Federal taxing power	28
1943	Prohibition of conditions in grants-in-aid	1
1943 to 1949	World federal government	6
1943 to 1947	Limitation of Presidential tenure	5
1945 to 1960	Treatymaking	6
1949	Tidelands problem	1
1952 and 1959	Preservation of States rights	2
1952	Distribution of proceeds of Federal taxes on gasoline	1
1952 to 1962	Repeal of 16th amendment	5
1953 to 1965	Revision of article V	13
1955 to 1965	Give States exclusive jurisdiction over public schools	3
1957	Balance of budget	1
1957 and 1961	Decisions of Supreme Court	3
1957	Oil and mineral rights	1

Dates	Subject matter of amendment proposed	Number of States submitting applications on subject
1957	Selection of Federal judges	1
1957 to 1969	Reapportionment	33
1958	State taxation power over income of nonresidents	1
1959	Constitutionality of 14th amendment	1
1959	Federal preemption	1
1963	Direct election of the President and Vice President	2
1963	Court of the Union	3
1963	National debt limit	1
1963 to 1966	Prayer in schools	3
1963	Taxation limit	1
1963	Electoral college	1
1963	Redistribution of presidential electors	2
1964	Pensions for persons over 65	1
1965	Presidential disability and succession	3
1965 to 1971	Return portion of Federal taxes to States Revenue sharing	15
1965	Equal rights for women	1
1965	Residence of Members of Congress	1
1965	Control Communist Party	1
1967	Permit Bible reading	1
1968	Limit tenure of Federal judges and Supreme Court justices	1
1968 to 1970	Permit freedom of choice in selection of schools	3
1970	Taxes—Income derived from interest	4
1970	To prohibit sedition and criminal anarchy	1
	Total	251

NOTE: A number of States have filed more than 1 petition on the same subject. This list does not include the additional petitions on the same subject.

Mr. ERVIN. Mr. President, today, as before, there are no rules on how such a convention should be called, how it should operate, or how it should be controlled. Most important, there is no law on the books that would confine a convention to a specific amendment. If we are to avoid the possibility of a runaway convention and a constitutional crisis, I believe it is imperative that orderly procedures be established for the conduct of a constitutional convention.

Why should this Nation go through crisis after crisis each time there is a new stirring among the States to propose a convention, for whatever purpose? It is the duty of Congress to specify the rules and the procedures, so that, if a constitutional convention is called, we shall be prepared to implement article V in an orderly and responsible manner. There is no need to subject Americans to the consternation which most certainly will be felt if the requisite 34 States petition for a convention.

Let me mention briefly the principal provisions of this legislation. S. 215 provides. . . .

That ratifications may be rescinded by the same process by which the amendment was ratified; except that a ratification may not be rescinded when there are valid ratifications by three-fourths of the States within the requisite time.

That when ratified, the Administrator of General Services shall issue a proclamation that the amendment is part of the Constitution.

c. EXCERPT FROM A LETTER FROM PAUL A. FREUND,
HARVARD LAW SCHOOL, DATED 3 JUNE 1971,
TO SENATOR PHILIP A. HART OF MICHIGAN
(117 *CONGRESSIONAL RECORD* 36762–63).

I am glad to reply to your letter inviting my comments on S. 215, relating to the procedures for the calling of a convention to propose constitutional amendments.

I agree with the sponsors of the bill that it will make a constructive contribution toward clarifying and regularizing a procedure that has received almost no attention hitherto. I also agree that Congress has the power to deal with this subject pursuant to Article V of the Constitution. If, as was stated in *Coleman* v. *Miller*, Congress may determine questions relating to ratification by virtue of its control over the promulgation of an amendment, it is much clearer that Congress possesses authority to regulate the procedures incident to a convention, since Article V gives Congress an explicit role in the calling of a convention though not in the stages of ratification or promulgation.

Let me turn to the specific points you have raised.

I am troubled by the provision that an application remains effective for seven years, though I recognize the force of symmetry in making this period parallel to that for ratification. The two stages, however, are not logically or practically equivalent. A case can be made for allowing a relatively long period for ratification after the Congress or a convention has performed the solemn deliberative act of proposing an amendment, while the call for a convention should stress more strongly the element of a contemporaneously felt need. I should think that a period of, say, four years would give adequate opportunity to the state legislatures to join in a request.

On the question of the time for rescission, I am inclined to go along with the Bill as drawn, lest an opportunity appear to be provided for delay in Congress with a view to stimulating rescissions before an actual call.

On the question of judicial review, I would expect the Court to hold that the issues are political and not justiciable, but I question the rather provocative form in which this concept is framed in the Bill. Instead of providing that the actions of Congress shall be binding on all others, including State and Federal courts, it could simply be stated that its decisions shall be final and binding. The legislative history could explain the meaning, including the point that judicial review is not contemplated, without raising what might appear to be a challenge to the courts. On the substance, I believe that it is wise to discourage review, though by phrasing the point less bluntly a slight opening might be left in case of some egregious action.

I would favor a two-thirds requirement for the vote in a convention, by analogy to the similar requirement for Congress.

I note that the Bill undertakes to deal with the question of ratification. As you know, the adoption of the Fourteenth Amendment involved an understanding that the States which had once rejected an amendment could ratify but that a ratification could not be rescinded. This seemed to me not illogical, since a rejection has no formal constitutional status while a ratification does. Nevertheless I would be prepared to accept the new rule for the future.

5. Duties of the General Services Administrator Regarding Constitutional Amendments

The following excerpt is from Title I United States Code.

106b. Amendments to Constitution.

Whenever official notice is received at the General Services Administration that any amendment proposed to the Constitution of the United States has been adopted, according to the provisions of the Constitution, the Administrator of General Services shall forthwith cause the amendment to be published, with his certificate, specifying the States by which the same may have been adopted, and that the same has become valid, to all intents and purposes, as a part of the Constitution of the United States. (Added Oct. 31, 1951, ch. 655, § 2 (b), 65 Stat. 710.)

6. Relevant Statutes and Resolutions

U.S. Senate debate on the attempted rescission of the Fourteenth Amendment by Ohio: *Cong. Globe,* 40th Cong., 2nd Sess. 876–78 (1868).

U.S. Senate debate on the adoption of the Fifteenth Amendment: *Cong. Globe,* 41st Cong., 2nd Sess. 377 (1870).

Declaration of secretary of state proclaiming the adoption of the Fifteenth Amendment: 16 Stat. 1131 (1870).

Declaration of secretary of state proclaiming the adoption of the Nineteenth Amendment: 41 Stat. 1823 (1920).

Transference of clerical duties from the secretary of state to the Administrator of General Services: Title 5 U.S.C. § 903 (1951).

1967 Ervin bill on constitutional conventions, S. 2307, 90th Cong., 1st Sess. (1967); not reported out of subcommittee.

1969 Ervin bill on constitutional conventions, S. 623, 91st Cong., 1st Sess. (1969); not reported out of full committee.

Connecticut's rejection of the state constitutional amendment to lower the voting age: *Statement of Vote: General Election November 3, 1970,* Pub. Doc. No. 26, State of Connecticut, p. 107.

Connecticut's ratification of the Twenty-sixth Amendment: S.J.R. No. 66 (1970).

1971 Ervin bill on constitutional conventions, S. 215, 92nd Cong., 1st Sess. (1971).

Report of Ervin subcommittee on separation of powers, S. Rep. No. 92–293, 92nd Cong., 1st Sess. (1971).

Amendment applications: 117 *Cong. Rec.* 36754 (1971).

Judiciary Committee hearings on 1971 Ervin Bill on constitutional conventions, H.R. 6919, 92nd Cong., 1st Sess. (1971).

Passage of ERA in Congress: 118 *Cong. Rec.* 9598 (1972).

1973 Ervin bill on constitutional conventions, S. 1272, 93rd Cong., 2nd Sess. (1973).

Nebraska's rescission resolution: 1973 Neb. Laws 1547 (Leg. Res. No. 9 adopted by 83rd Leg., 1st Sess., 15 March 1973).

Judiciary Committee hearings on 1973 Ervin bill on constitutional conventions, H.J.R. 827, 93rd Cong., 2nd Sess. (1973).

Tennessee's rescission resolution: S.J. Res. 29, 88th Gen. Assembly (1974).

Idaho's referendum provision: Idaho Code § 34–2217 (1975).

Idaho's rescission resolution: H.C.R. 10–950 Id. Sess. Laws (adopted by 44th Leg., 1st Sess., 8 February 1977).

Appendix D

Opinions of Constitutional Scholars

1. Senator Sam J. Ervin, Jr.

a. EXCERPT FROM LETTER TO SAMUEL S. FREEDMAN.

Senator Ervin sent copies of his several statements concerning ERA to Samuel S. Freedman with a covering letter dated 8 March 1977. The following excerpt is from that letter.

In a letter which I wrote to Mrs. Irene Bella Donna of Fairfield, Connecticut on February 11, I gave a complete analysis of the case of *Coleman v. Miller*. I also alluded to the Coleman Case in a statement which I sent to the members of the North Carolina State Senate. Copies of both of these statements are enclosed.

In addition to discussing the Coleman Case, the last statement also points out that the Legislature of a State has the right to either ratify an Amendment which it has rejected or to rescind a ratification it has made at any time before three-fourths of the States have ratified the Amendment, and thus placed it beyond the power of a State Legislature to change its mind.

There is no authority to this effect. However, reason compels its acceptance.

As I read *Leser v. Garnett*, the Supreme Court held in that case that there was nothing in the Constitution to prevent Congress and the States from submitting and ratifying the Nineteenth Amendment, that laws of the States could not impair the powers of States to ratify a proposed Amendment, and that the Secretary of State, who then had the duty to certify whether a proposed consitutional Amendment had been ratified by the requisite number of States, would not go behind the certificate of a particular state certifying that it had ratified a proposed Amendment.

I do not think there is anything in *Leser v. Garnett* which militates against my position. On the contrary, the Administrator of the General Services Administration, who has now succeeded to the duty of the Secretary of State, would have to certify the certificates from the States, and it would be his duty to accept the last of these certificates. Hence, it is in favor of those who maintain that a State which has ratified can rescind its ratification by a subsequent resolution.

I construe Title 1 U.S.C.A. Sec. 106(b) to be merely a statute transferring from the Secretary of the State to the Administrator of General Services the duty of making the certificate of ratification.

I certainly do not construe it to deny the Courts the power to go behind a false certificate made by the Administrator of General Services. It would be intolerable in our system of government for one individual, to wit, the Administrator of General Services, to add an Amendment to the Constitution upon ratification of less than three-fourths of the States by making a false statement.

As I indicate in my statements, a Supreme Court which has rendered the decision in *Baker v. Carr* and *Powell v. McCormick* will never hold that the question of whether a constitutional Amendment has been ratified is a political question for the determination of Congress rather than a judicial question for the determination of the Supreme Court.

I cannot imagine any question involving an interpretation of the Constitution which is more important than the question of whether an Amendment to the Constitution has been ratified. Hence, I believe that States which rescind a previous ratification can be sure that the Supreme Court will decide the validity of their rescission.

b. STATEMENT OF SAM J. ERVIN, JR. CONCERNING LATE ARGUMENTS OF ADVOCATES OF ERA (26 FEBRUARY 1977).

In a desperate effort to persuade members of the State Senate to refuse to permit their constituents to express their opinion on ERA in a state-wide referendum, advocates of the ERA present at the last hour these specious arguments:

1. That a State which has ratified the ERA cannot rescind its ratification.

2. That the North Carolina Legislature does not have the power to submit the ERA to a referendum because it is not expressly authorized to do so by either the Constitution of the United States or the Constitution of North Carolina.

There is no valid argument to support either of these allegations.

The argument that a State which has rejected ERA can thereafter ratify it, and that a State which has ratified ERA cannot thereafter rescind its ratification rests merely upon the erroneous construction placed by some unqualified persons on the Supreme Court decision in *Coleman v. Miller,* 307 U.S. 433, which was handed down in 1939 by a Supreme Court whose Justices were hopelessly split into three irreconcilable groups.

Coleman v. Miller did not decide anything except the proposition that whether Kansas had the power to ratify the proposed child labor amendment after previously rejecting it was a political question for the determination of Congress and not a judicial question for the determination of the Supreme Court.

In the final result, the *Coleman Case* really decides nothing because anyone who reads such subsequent Supreme Court cases as *Baker v. Carr,* 369 U.S. 186, and *Powell v. McCormick,* 395 U.S. 483, knows that the present Supreme Court will never hold that the interpretation of the Constitution is a political question and not a judicial question.

The invalidity of the first argument is demonstrated beyond question by a rule of law which is universally recognized throughout the United States. Under this rule, one Legislature cannot tie either its own hands or those of its successors with respect to subjects on which they have the power to act. What they do today, they can undo tomorrow, and what they refuse to do today, they can do tomorrow.

Hence, the Legislature may consider and reconsider, and ratify or rescind ratification of a proposed Amendment to the United States Constitution as often as they see fit until the proposed Amendment becomes a part of the Constitution by its final ratification by three-fourths of the States. Then and only then does the Legislature lose its power to change its mind in respect to any proposed Amendment to the United States Constitution.

The second argument is equally as invalid. It is based upon a distinct misunderstanding of the nature of the constitutional system under which the North Carolina Legislature acts.

Under our constitutional system, the Legislature of North Carolina can do whatever it wishes to do about anything unless its action is forbidden by the Federal or State Constitutions.

There is not a syllable in either of these Constitutions which forbids the North Carolina Legislature to refer the ERA to the people to ascertain whether they want it.

The North Carolina Legislature has submitted many legislative proposals, such as the proposal to establish the State Ports Authority and the act authorizing the issuance of bonds and loans to veterans for the construction of homes, in referendums to the people.

Moreover, the submission to a referendum of a proposed constitutional amendment is no new thing. By Act of Congress and by Act of the North Carolina Legislature, the constitutional amendment to repeal the 18th Amendment was submitted to the vote of the people of North Carolina. To be sure, this particular referendum was final. The proposed referendum of the ERA would be subject to the subsequent action of the North Carolina Legislature after they have ascertained the will of the people in respect to ERA.

We have just completed our Bicentennial year. Have the advocates of the ERA forgotten so quickly that the Declaration of Independence proclaims what all of us profess to believe—that all the just powers of government are derived from the people.

Why are the advocates of ERA so afraid of the people?

c. STATEMENT OF SAM J. ERVIN, JR. CONCERNING THE BIZARRE AND SPECIOUS CLAIM OF SUPPORTERS OF THE EQUAL RIGHTS AMENDMENT THAT A STATE WHICH HAS REJECTED THE AMENDMENT CAN CHANGE ITS MIND AND VOTE TO RATIFY, WHEREAS A STATE WHICH HAS RATIFIED THE AMENDMENT CANNOT CHANGE ITS MIND AND VOTE TO RESCIND OR WITHDRAW ITS RATIFICATION.

1. *Several States have voted to rescind or withdraw their previous ratifications of the ERA. Other States are seriously considering doing likewise. To deter the other States from exercising their right to rescind or withdraw their previous ratifications of the Amendment, supporters of the Amendment are now making the bizarre and specious claim that a State which has rejected the Amendment may change its mind and vote to ratify whereas a State which has ratified cannot change its mind and vote to rescind or withdraw its ratification. For reasons hereafter stated, the claim lacks credible support in authority and reason.*

Idaho, Nebraska, and Tennessee have voted to rescind or withdraw their previous ratifications of ERA. Other States are seriously considering doing likewise.

To deceive state legislators who are contemplating such action into believing that they have no power to do so, and thus deter them from rescinding or withdrawing their previous ratification of the Amendment, supporters of ERA are now vociferously claiming that a state which has rejected the Amendment can change its mind and vote to ratify whereas a state which has ratified cannot change its mind and vote to rescind or withdraw its previous ratification.

Insofar as fairness is concerned, this claim is on a par with the ''I win and you lose'' proposal of the coin-tossing gambler; and insofar as logic is concerned, it is on a par with the proposition that what is sauce for the legislative goose is not sauce for the legislative gambler.

In the last analysis, the advocates of ERA base their bizarre and specious claim upon the supposition that it finds support in the decision of the Supreme Court of the United States in *Coleman v. Miller*, (1937) 307 U.S. 433, 83 L.Ed. 1385, 59 S.Ct. 972, 122 A.L.R. 695.

As one who has studied this question ever since I began to formulate with the aid of the most knowledgeable constitutional scholars in America a bill to establish procedures to govern a constitutional convention called by Congress on the application of the legislatures of two-thirds of the states pursuant to the alternative method authorized by Article V of the Constitution of the United States, I assert without fear of successful contradiction that the *Coleman Case* decided nothing of the kind, and that in consequence those ERA supporters who make this claim have no foundation for it in authority or reason.

I digress to point out that my bill, which passed the Senate virtually without opposition on several occasions, expressly authorized states which had ratified a proposed amendment to rescind their previous ratification "provided the ratifications of three-fourths of the states had not yet been secured." (See C. Herman Pritchett, "The American Constitution", page 40)

2. The question whether a state which has ratified a proposed amendment to the Federal Constitution can change its mind and vote to rescind or withdraw its ratification was not even involved in the Coleman Case. Moreover, the question whether a state which has rejected a proposed amendment can change its mind and vote to ratify was not decided in the Coleman Case. On the contrary, the Supreme Court of the United States invoked the "political question" doctrine in the Coleman Case and adjudged that this question is a political matter for the determination of Congress and not a judicial matter for the decision of the Court.

The facts in the *Coleman Case* were simple. In 1924 Congress proposed an amendment to the Federal Constitution known as the Child Labor Amendment. The resolution submitting it to the states did not limit the time for its ratification. In 1925, the Kansas Legislature rejected it. In 1937, however, a resolution to ratify the Amendment was introduced in the Kansas State Senate, where twenty Senators voted for the resolution and twenty voted against it. The Lieutenant Governor of Kansas, the presiding officer of the Senate, then cast his vote in favor of the resolution. The resolution was later adopted by the Kansas House of Representatives on the vote of a majority of its members.

The twenty Senators who had voted against the resolution and three Representatives then brought an original action in the Supreme Court of Kansas seeking a mandamus to compel the Secretary of the Kansas Senate to record that the resolution had not passed and to restrain the officials of the Legislature from signing the resolution and the Secretary of State of Kansas from certifying it to the Governor.

These Senators and Representatives assailed the attempted ratification of the Child Labor Amendment on these grounds: (1) that the Amendment had been previously rejected by the Kansas Legislature; (2) that it was no longer open to ratification because an unreasonable time, thirteen years, had elapsed since Congress had submitted it to the States; and (3) that the Lieutenant Governor had no right to cast the deciding vote in the Kansas Senate in favor of ratification.

The Supreme Court of Kansas rejected these contentions and upheld the ratification of the Amendment on the ground that a state legislature which has rejected an amendment proposed by Congress may later ratify it.

I digress to observe that this ruling was in accord with the universally accepted principle that a legislative body cannot tie the hands of its successors.

The Supreme Court of the United States, which granted certiorari, split into three irreconcilable groups, who wrote four opinions.

Upon two preliminary questions somewhat procedural in nature, i.e., whether the Supreme Court of the United States had jurisdiction to review the rulings of the Kansas Court, and whether the twenty Kansas Senators had standing to sue, the Justices split five to four.

Chief Justice Hughes and Justices Stone and Reed, who adhered to Chief Justice Hughes' so-called majority opinion, and the two dissenting Justices, McReynolds and Butler, held that the Supreme Court of the United States had jurisdiction and that the twenty Kansas State Senators had standing to sue.

The other four Justices, Roberts, Black, Frankfurter, and Douglas, who adhered to the two opinions written by Black and Frankfurter, disagreed with them because of their view that Congress possesses exclusive power under Article V of the Constitution over the entire amending process and in consequence "neither state nor federal courts can review [the exercise] of that power." (307 U.S. 433, 459)

With respect to a more substantive question, i.e., whether the Lieutenant Governor had the power to cast the deciding vote in favor of ratification, Chief Justice Hughes had this to say: "Whether this contention presents a justiciable controversy, or a question which is political in nature, and hence not justiciable, is a question upon which the Court is equally divided, and therefore the Court expresses no opinion upon that point." (307 U.S. 433, 447)

It is regrettable that Chief Justice Hughes did not reveal the mystery of how nine or five Justices could be "equally divided" on a constitutional question. In the absence of any such revelation, one is compelled to conclude that one of the Justices was suffering a species of intellectual schizophrenia which disabled him to ascertain the con[s]ensus of his own mind.

The Justices split into three irreconcilable groups upon these two remaining questions:

1. Whether a state which had rejected the Child Labor Amendment could subsequently change its mind and vote to ratify it; and,

2. Whether the Child Labor Amendment was no longer open to ratification because an unreasonable time had elapsed since Congress had submitted it to the states.

When the *Coleman Case* is read in its entirety, it is obvious that the Supreme Court divided on these questions in this fashion:

1. Chief Justice Hughes and Justices Stone and Reed concluded that these questions were political questions for determination by Congress and not judicial questions for the decision of Courts. (307 U.S. 433, 436–457)

2. Justices McReynolds and Butler concluded that the Supreme Court of the United States had judicial power to adjudge and ought to adjudge that the Kansas Legislature had no power to ratify the Child Labor Amendment because an unreasonable time had elapsed since Congress had submitted it to the States. (308 U.S. 433, 470–474)

3. Justices Roberts, Black, Frankfurter, and Douglas concluded that the Supreme Court of the United States was powerless to make any pronouncement in respect to either question because Article V of the Federal Constitution had committed complete and unreviewable power over the entire amending power to Congress. (307 U.S. 433, 456–470)

These diverse conclusions compelled the affirmance of the ruling of the Kansas Supreme Court. In taking such action, Chief Justice Hughes made it plain that the Supreme Court of the United States was not expressing any opinion as to the validity of the basis of the Kansas Court's decision, i.e., that a state legislature which has rejected an amendment proposed by Congress can change its mind and ratify it. He did this by expressly stating that the Supreme Court was affirming the ruling solely ''upon the grounds stated in this opinion.'' (307 U.S. 433, 456)

The only allusion in the *Coleman Case* to the question whether a state which has ratified a proposed amendment can change its mind and rescind or withdraw its ratification is in the form of dicta, which puts the questions of ratification after rejection and rescission or withdrawal after ratifying in the same category and which appears in this sentence:

''We think that in accordance with this historic precedent the question of the efficacy of ratifications by state legislatures, in the light of previous rejection or attempted withdrawal, should be regarded as a political question pertaining to the political departments, with the ultimate authority in Congress in the exercise of its control over the promulgation of the adoption of the amendment.'' (307 U.S. 433, 450)

As one who loves constitutional government, I must confess that I am abhorred by the proposition that Congress has complete and unreviewable power to control the amending process in all its stages. This proposition would permit a false decision by a partisan or radical Congress to rob the people, the states, and the courts of their power to enforce constitutional government in our land.

3. *All credible commentators agree that the Coleman Case does not support the bizarre and specious claim of the supporters of ERA that a state which has rejected the Amendment can change its mind and vote to ratify whereas a state which has ratified cannot change its mind and vote to rescind or withdraw its ratification.*

In preparing this statement, I read the *Coleman Case* many times. Moreover, I consulted comments on it in these publications: the first and only edition (1969) of *Modern Constitutional Law*, which was written by Chester J. Antieau, Professor of Constitutional Law at Georgetown University; the second and last edition (1968) of *The American Constitution*, which was written by C. Herman Pritchett, Professor of Political Science at the University of Chicago; the numerous editions (1920 through 1974) of *The Constitution And What It Means Today*, which was originally written by Edward S. Corwin, of Princeton University, and which has been revised by others since his death; and the various editions of the *Constitution of the United States, Revised and Annotated*, which was originally compiled and edited by Edward S. Corwin and which has been printed by the authority of Congress.

All of these authorities share my conviction that the Supreme Court of the United States did not decide anything whatever in the *Coleman Case* beyond some procedural questions immaterial to our present concern except the proposition that whether a state legislature has ratified a proposed amendment to the Federal Constitution is a political question for the decision of Congress and not a judicial question for the decision of the courts.

I quote their interpretations of the meaning of the *Coleman Case*.

Professor Antieau quotes this crucial passage from the so-called majority opinion in the *Coleman Case*: "The question of the efficacy of ratifications by state legislatures, *in the light of previous rejection or attempted withdrawal*, should be regarded as a political question pertaining to the political departments, with the ultimate authority in the Congress, in the exercise of its control over the promulgation of the amendment." On the basis of the opinion and decision conforming to the view thus expressed, Professor Antieau interpreted the holding in the *Coleman Case* to be as follows:

"Whether a state has ratified or rejected an amendment to the Federal Constitution is a political question for Congress to decide, and the federal courts will not determine the same. . . . What rules Congress will adopt is not yet obvious.'' *Antieau: Modern Constitutional Law*, Vol. 2, Section 12:178, pages 485–486.

By his statement "what rules Congress will adopt is not yet obvious," Professor Antieau asserts, in effect, that there is nothing whatever to indicate what Congress will decide in respect to a previous rejection of a proposed amendment or an attempted withdrawal of a previous ratification. Hence, he declares, in essence, that there is no foundation for the claim of the supporters of ERA in the event the Supreme Court should adhere to the ruling that the question is a political question for Congress and not a judicial question for the court.

Professor Pritchett said that "in *Coleman v. Miller* the Supreme Court said" that the action of the state legislature in respect to a proposed amendment to the Federal Constitution "should be regarded as a political matter with the ultimate authority of decision in Congress." *C. Herman Pritchett: The American Constitution*, page 40.

Professor Corwin said:

> "From the opinions filed in the case of *Coleman v. Miller*, in 1939, in which certain questions were raised concerning the status of the proposed Child Labor Amendment (pending since 1924) it would seem that the Court today regards all questions relating to the interpretation" of Article V of the Constitution of the United States "as political questions, and hence addressed exclusively to Congress." *Edward S. Corwin: The Constitution And What It Means Today*, page 219.

After giving the correct interpretation to the *Coleman Case* that the Supreme Court decided nothing in it except that whether the Kansas Legislature could ratify the Child Labor Amendment after rejecting it, Professor Corwin made this contradictory and confusing statement:

> "If a state legislature ratifies a proposed amendment may it later reconsider its vote, the amendment not having yet received the favorable vote of three-fourths of the legislatures? In *Coleman v. Miller* this question was answered 'No' on the basis of Congressional Rulings in connection with the adoption of the Fourteenth Amendment. May a legislature, after rejecting a proposed amendment, reconsider and ratify it? On the same basis, this question was answered 'Yes' in Coleman v. Miller.'' *Edward S. Corwin: The Constitution And What It Means Today*, page 220.

This contradictory and confusing statement is the only authority I have been able to find for the whimsically strange assertion of the ERA supporters that a state which has rejected can ratify whereas a state which has ratified cannot rescind its ratification.

In addition to being irreconcilable with his own preceding interpretation of the *Coleman Case*, Professor Corwin's second statement is without merit for these reasons:

1. The court did not answer "No" or anything else in the *Coleman Case* to the question whether a state which has ratified a proposed amendment can change its mind and rescind or withdraw its ratification. The court did not and could not answer that question in the *Coleman Case* because it did not arise in that case. In the portion of his opinion quoted by Professor Antieau and set forth above, Chief Justice Hughes alluded to the question by way of dicta when he said, in effect, that the question of the efficacy of an "attempted withdrawal" of a previous ratification as well as the question of the efficacy of a subsequent ratification after a "previous rejection" were political questions for Congress and not judicial questions for the courts.

2. The court did not answer "yes" or anything else in the *Coleman Case* to the question whether a state which has rejected a proposed amendment can change its mind and ratify it. Although the Kansas Supreme Court had based its decision upholding the vote of the Kansas legislature ratifying the Child Labor Amendment after a previous rejection upon the view that "a state legislature which has rejected an amendment proposed by Congress may later ratify", the Supreme Court refused to make any such ruling on the ground that the question of the efficacy of the action of the Kansas legislature was a political question for the determination of Congress and not a judicial question for the decision of the Court. Indeed, the Supreme Court even refused to endorse the basis on which the Kansas Supreme Court made its ruling. As appears by the opinion of Chief Justice Hughes in the *Coleman Case* (307 U.S. 433, 456), the Supreme Court of the United States affirmed the judgment of the Kansas Supreme Court upon the grounds stated by Chief Justice Hughes and not for the reasons given by the Kansas Supreme Court.

Professor Corwin's "Yes" and "No" aberration is traceable to the concurrent resolution which Congress adopted on July 21, 1868, and which Chief Justice Hughes cited for precedential support for the unprecedented judicial ruling in the *Coleman Case* that the question whether the Kansas legislature had the power to ratify the Child Labor Amendment after previously rejecting it was a political question for Congress and not a judicial question for the Courts.

To understand why Professor Corwin deemed this resolution a precedent for his "Yes" and "No" proposition, we must know some facts not disclosed by it.

In 1868, Congress was dominated by huge majorities of radicals, who had passed the notorious Reconstruction Acts over President Andrew Johnson's vetoes, and who were bent above all things in putting the proposed Fourteenth Amendment into effect without delay to better their prospects in the approaching fall election.

All of the Southern States except Tennessee had previously rejected the proposed Fourteenth Amendment. An irritated Congress decreed that these states would have no representation in the United States Congress until they adopted new state constitutions conforming to the Reconstruction Acts and ratified the Fourteenth Amendment.

Since the states then numbered 37, ratification of the proposed Fourteenth Amendment by three-fourths of them, i.e., 28, was required by Article V to make the Amendment a part of the Constitution.

As a result of the congressional coercion, the number of ratifying states had risen to 29 by early July, 1868. Two of them, Ohio and New Jersey, however, had voted to rescind or withdraw their ratifications.

An impatient Congress ignored the action of Ohio and New Jersey and adopted its concurrent resolution of July 21, 1868, declaring that 29 states, including Ohio and New Jersey, had ratified the Fourteenth Amendment and made it a part of the Constitution. At least two of the states, North Carolina and South Carolina, which were enumerated by the resolution among the 29 ratifying states, had previously rejected the Amendment.

While an impatient Congress was taking this precipitate action on the day stated, another state, Georgia, ratified the Fourteenth Amendment and thus made the question of the constitutionality of the ignoring of the rescissions or withdrawals of Ohio and New Jersey moot.

This is the shaky basis on which Professor Corwin's "Yes" and "No" aberration rested. An impatient Congress merely ignored what had happened. It did not adjudge that Ohio and New Jersey lacked the power to rescind or withdraw their ratifications.

And even if Congress had done so, its action would be destitute of precedential force under the well established constitutional principle that one Congress cannot tie the hands of a succeeding Congress. *Reichelderfer v. Quinn* (1932), 287 U.S. 315, 77 L.Ed. 331, 53 S.Ct. 177, 83 A.L.R. 1429.

Professor Corwin inserted his "Yes" and "No" aberration in the first revision of his book appearing after the decision in the *Coleman Case*. It was repeated without change in subsequent revisions.

Fortunately for the triumph of truth, Professor Corwin made it clear that his "Yes" and "No" aberration did not constitute any part of the decision in the *Coleman Case* when he subsequently compiled and edited the *Constitution of the United States of America, Revised and Annotated*, for the Congress. I quote his words:

> "Prior to 1939, the Supreme Court had taken cognizance of a number of diverse objections to the validity of specific amendments. Apart from holding that official notice of ratification by the several states was conclusive upon the courts, it had treated the questions as justiciable, although it had uniformly rejected them on the merits. In that year, however, the whole subject was thrown into confusion by the inconclusive decision in *Coleman v. Miller*. This case came up on a writ of

certiorari to the Supreme Court of Kansas to review the denial of a writ of mandamus to compel the Secretary of the Kansas Senate to erase an endorsement on a resolution ratifying the proposed child labor amendment to the Constitution to the effect that it had been adopted by the Kansas State Senate. The attempted ratification was assailed on three grounds: (1) that the amendment had been previously rejected by the state legislature; (2) that it was no longer open to ratification because an unreasonable period of time, thirteen years, had elapsed since its submission to the states; and (3) that the Lieutenant Governor had no right to cast the deciding vote in the Kansas Senate in favor of ratification.

"Four opinions were written in the Supreme Court, no one of which commanded the support of more than four members of the Court. The majority ruled that the plaintiffs, members of the Kansas States Senate, had a sufficient interest in the controversy to give the federal courts jurisdiction to review the case. Without agreement with regard to the grounds for their decision, a different majority affirmed the judgment of the Kansas Court denying the relief sought. Four members who concurred in the result had voted to dismiss the writ on the ground that the amending process is 'political in its entirety, from submission until an amendment becomes a part of the Constitution, and is not subject to judicial guidance, control, or interference at any point.' Whether the contention that the Lieutenant Governor should have been permitted to cast the deciding vote in favor of ratification presented a justiciable controversy was left undecided, the Court being equally divided on the point. In an opinion reported as 'the opinion of the Court', but in which it appears that only three Justices concurred, *Chief Justice Hughes declared that the writ of mandamus was properly denied because the question as to the effect of the previous rejection of the amendment and the lapse of time since it was submitted to the states were political questions which should be left to Congress." Constitution of the United States, Revised and Annotated, 1972,* pages 860–861.

Hence, Professor Corwin's own words reveal that his final interpretation of the *Coleman Case* is identical with that placed upon it by me in section 2 of this statement.

4. *The only reasonable interpretation of Article V of the Constitution, which governs the amendatory process, is that it authorizes a state which has rejected a proposed amendment to change its mind and vote to ratify the same and permits a state which has ratified a proposed amendment to change its mind and rescind or withdraw its ratification at any time before three-fourths of the states have voted to ratify the proposed amendment and thus made it a part of the Constitution. This view rejects the unfair and illogical claim of the advocates of ERA, and permits the states to continue the search for truth until the amendatory process is consummated. And this is so regardless of whether the resultant questions are political questions for Congress or judicial questions for the courts.*

I have called attention in other sections of this statement to the bizarre claim of advocates of ERA that a state legislature which has rejected the Amendment may change its mind and vote to ratify it, but a state legislature which has ratified the Amendment cannot change its mind and vote to rescind or withdraw its ratification. They cannot explain in a rational manner why they think the Constitution of the United States grants freedom to some legislative bodies, and imprisons others in mental jails.

They invoke their bizarre claim because they understandably fear that if state legislatures which ratified ERA in haste and under their pressure are permitted to exercise their intelligence and re-examine and re-appraise ERA, they may decide to repent in wisdom of what they did in folly and vote to correct their mistake.

Other Americans, who cannot accept the arbitrary, unfair, illogical, and tyrannical view of advocates of ERA, have advanced two other views in respect to the power state legislatures may exercise in the amendatory process under Article V of the United States Constitution, which authorizes Congress and the states to amend the Constitution and prescribes the process by which they must act to exercise this awesome power.

For ease of statement, I shall call one of these views the Kentucky view, and the other the view shared by multitudes of other Americans and me.

The Court of Appeals of Kentucky expressed the Kentucky view in *Wise v. Chandler*, (1937), 270 Ky. 1, 108 S.W.2d 1024, which held that if a state rejects a proposed amendment it cannot later ratify the same, unless it is resubmitted by Congress.

The Kentucky Court justified its ruling in this way: "We think the conclusion is inescapable that a state can act but once, either by convention or through its legislature, upon a proposed amendment; and whether its vote be in the affirmative or the negative, having acted, it has exhausted its power further to consider the question without a resubmission by Congress." *Chester J. Antieau: Modern Constitutional Law*, Vol. 2, Section 12:178.

The view shared by multitudes of other Americans and me may be stated in this fashion:

A state legislature does not forfeit its liberty of thought or action as long as the amendatory process is incomplete by either ratifying or rejecting a proposed amendment to the Constitution of the United States. Hence, a state legislature which has rejected a proposed amendment may change its mind and ratify it, and a state legislature which has ratified a proposed amendment may change its mind and rescind or withdraw its ratification at any time before three-fourths of the states have ratified the amendment and thus made it a part of the Constitution. *Chester J. Antieau: Modern Constitutional Law*, Vol. 2, Section 12:178; *C. Herman Pritchett: The American Constitution*, pages 39–40.

On the day of its unprecedented decision in the *Coleman Case*, the Supreme Court of the United States, by a seven to two vote of the Justices, dismissed without decision the writ of certiorari previously granted by it to review the ruling of the Kentucky Court in *Wise v. Chandler* on the ground that it no longer presented a justiciable controversy susceptible of judicial determination. *Chandler v. Wise*, (1939), 207 U.S. 474, 83 L.Ed 1407.

If we are to appraise aright the role of state legislatures in the amendatory process, we must read Article V of the United States Constitution in the light of the rules devised by experience, reason, and law to enable state legislatures to perform their functions in civil government.

Article V proclaims:

"The Congress, whenever two thirds of both Houses shall deem it necessary, shall propose Amendments to this Constitution, or, on the application of the Legislatures of two thirds of the several states, shall call a Convention for proposing Amendments, which in either case, shall be valid to all intents and purposes, as part of this Constitution, when ratified by the Legislatures of three-fourths of the several states or by Conventions in three-fourths thereof, as the one or the other mode of ratification may be proposed by the Congress; Provided that no Amendment which may be made prior to the year one thousand eight hundred and eight shall in any manner affect the first and fourth clauses in the ninth section of the first Article; and that no state, without its consent, shall be deprived of its equal suffrage in the Senate."

No intelligent American will gainsay the proposition that voting to amend the Constitution of the United States is the most crucial task a state legislator can perform. This is true because an amendment to the Federal Constitution will control the lives of all generations of Americans as long as time shall last unless it is sooner removed from that instrument by another Amendment.

With the exception of the proviso making secure the right of each state to equal suffrage in the Senate, there is not a syllable in Article V which undertakes to put any limitation whatever upon what state legislatures can do in their amendatory role except the implied limitation that they can not effectively act after a proposed amendment has been ratified by three-fourths of the states and made a part of the Constitution.

On the contrary, except for the proviso stated, every word of Article V is in complete harmony with these conclusions: (1) A state legislature does not forfeit its liberty of thought or action as long as the amendatory process is incomplete by either ratifying or rejecting a proposed amendment to the Constitution of the United States; and (2) hence, a state legislature which has rejected a proposed amendment may change its mind and ratify it, and a state legislature which has ratified a proposed amendment can change its mind and rescind or withdraw its ratification.

These conclusions are inescapable. Moreover, they are inseparable from the spirit and purpose of Article V, which clearly contemplates that state legislators shall act with complete liberty of spirit and complete freedom of mind as long as state legislatures are participating in the amendatory process.

The rules devised by experience, reason, and law to enable state legislatures in America to perform their functions in civil government are well established in all areas of our land. They are two-fold in nature, and may be stated with simplicity as follows:

1. A state legislature may do what the state and federal Constitutions do not forbid it to do.

16 Am. Jur. 2d, Constitutional Law, Section 228.

72 Am. Jur. 2d, States, Sections 40, 41.

73 Am. Jur. 2d, Statutes, Section 33.

Giozza v. Tiernan (1893), 148 U.S. 657, 37 L.Ed. 599, 13 S.Ct. 721.

Chicago, Burlington and Quincy Railroad v. County of Otoe (1873), 16 Wall. (U.S.) 667, 21 L.Ed. 375.

Ware v. Hylton (1796), 3 Dall. (U.S.) 199, 1 L.Ed. 568.

Lassiter v. Northampton County Board of Elections (1948), 248 U.S. N.C.102, 102 S.E.2d 853, affirmed 360 U.S. 45, 3 L.Ed.2d 1072, 79 S.Ct. 985.

Village of North Atlanta v. Cook, (1963), 219 Ga. 316, 133 S.E.2d 585, 589.

2. A state legislature cannot restrict or limit the right of a succeeding legislature to exercise its constitutional power in its own way. In other words, it cannot tie the hands of its successors.

72 Am. Jur. 2d, States, Section 40.

73 Am. Jur. 2d, Statutes, Section 34.

Stone v. Mississippi (1880), 101 U.S. 814, 25 L.Ed. 1079.

Newton v. Mahoning County (1880) 100 U.S. 548, 25 L.Ed. 710.

Boston Beer Co. v. Massachusetts (1878), 97 U.S. 25, 24 L.Ed. 989.

Bank of Columbia v. Okely (1819), 4 Wheat. (U.S.) 235, 4 L.Ed. 557.

Fletcher v. Peck (1810), 6 Cranch (U.S.) 87, 3 L.Ed. 162.

State v. Wall (1967) 271 N.C. 675, 683, 157 S.E.2d 363.

Kornegay v. City of Goldsboro (1920), 180 N.C. 441, 105 S.E. 187.

Village of North Atlanta v. Cook (1963), 219 Ga. 316, 133 S.E.2d 585, 589.

What has been said makes these things plain:

1. The claim of ERA supporters that a state which has ratified the Amendment cannot rescind or withdraw its ratification is totally repugnant

to Article V and the rules devised by experience, reason, and law to enable state legislatures to perform their functions in civil government.

2. Although it is impartial and logical, the Kentucky view is inconsistent with Article V because it prohibits further activity by ratifying and rejecting states while the amendatory process is still going on.

3. The view shared by multitudes of other Americans and me is in complete harmony with Article V and the rules devised by experience, reason, and law to enable state legislatures to perform their functions in civil government. Hence, this view is the sound one.

5. *If the Supreme Court should adhere to its unprecedented ruling in the Coleman Case, Congress will be obligated to judge the question of whether ERA has been ratified by the true meaning of Article V, which is that a state legislature has power to ratify ERA after having previously rejected it and that a state legislature has power to rescind or withdraw its ratification of ERA after having previously ratified it. Since reason, the Constitution and prior Supreme Court decisions compel the conclusion that whether a proposed amendment to the Federal Constitution has been ratified in conformity with Article V is rightly a judicial question, and since subsequent Supreme Court decisions disclose the existing tendency of the Supreme Court to narrow the "political-question doctrine", it seems probable that the Supreme Court will return to its former position and hold that whether ERA has been ratified is a judicial question for its ultimate decision.*

The *Coleman Case* is unprecedented. Moreover, it is contrary to six prior decisions of the Supreme Court, which covered the first 150 years of the nation's history, and which recognized and applied the sound constitutional principle that the question whether a proposed amendment to the Constitution of the United States has been ratified in conformity to Article V is a judicial question for the ultimate decision of the Supreme Court itself. I cite these six cases below.

> *United States v. Sprague* (1931), 282 U.S. 716, 75 L.Ed. 640, 51 S.Ct. 220, 71 A.L.R. 1381.
>
> *Leser v. Garnett*, (1922) 258 U.S. 130, 66 L.Ed. 606, 43 S.Ct. 217.
>
> *Dillon v. Gloss* (1921), 256 U.S. 368, 65 L.Ed. 994, 41 S.Ct. 510.
>
> *Hawke v. Smith* (1920), 253 U.S. 221, 64 L.Ed. 877, 40 S.Ct. 498.
>
> *National Prohibition Cases*, (1920) 253 U.S. 350, 64 L.Ed. 946, 40 S.Ct. 486 (Note: Reported as Rhode Island v. Palmer)
>
> *Hollingsworth v. Virginia*, (1798) 3 Dall. 378, 1 L.Ed. 644.

It is to be noted that the Supreme Court exercised jurisdiction in these cases after the Secretary of State had proclaimed that the Amendment assailed had been ratified by three-fourths of the states. This simple ministerial function has since been transferred to the Administrator of General Services by 1 *U.S.C.A.* 106b.

If the Supreme Court should adhere to its unprecedented ruling in the *Coleman Case* that questions of the validity of votes of state legislatures engaged in the amendatory process under Article V are political rather than judicial questions under the "political-question doctrine", Congress should be required by the oath of its members to support the Constitution to recognize and implement the true meaning of Article V, which is that a state legislature has power to ratify ERA after having previously rejected it and that a state legislature has power to rescind or withdraw its ratification of ERA after having previously ratified it. Any other Congressional conclusion would be faithless to Article V.

Sound reason compels the deliberate conclusion that the holding in the *Coleman Case* constitutes a temporary judicial aberration, and that the Supreme Court will welcome an opportunity to return to its original position, i.e., that questions concerning the ratification of proposed amendments to the Federal Constitution are judicial questions for the ultimate decision of the Supreme Court in accordance with the provisions of Article V.

I set forth below the basis for this observation.

Under Section 2 of Article III of the Constitution, the judicial power of the United States extends to all cases arising under the Constitution, and various Acts of Congress grant the District Courts of the United States original jurisdiction to try such cases and the Courts of Appeal and the Supreme Court of the United States appellate jurisdiction to review the trial of such cases.

Undoubtedly, the most important case which can arise under the Constitution is one involving the question whether that instrument has been changed in the only way in which it can be changed, i.e., by an amendment which has been ratified by three-fourths of the states.

The phraseology of Article III and the Acts of Congress implementing such Article undoubtedly suffice to vest in the courts of the United States jurisdiction to hear and determine cases of this nature, and such Courts did in fact exercise such jurisdiction without question and with the complete satisfaction to the nation during the 150 years after the Constitution became effective.

On June 5, 1939, however, the Supreme Court turned its back on the words of Article III and the Acts of Congress implementing them and 150 years of its own history and adjudged that a case of this nature is a political question for Congress and not a judicial question for it.

These naked facts indicate that the Supreme Court had some difficulty in reaching this strange decision: the case was argued October 10, 1938; it was restored to the docket for re-argument January 30, 1939; it was reargued April 17 and 18, 1939; and it was finally decided on June 5, 1939 by Justices hopelessly split into three irreconcilable groups, no group constituting a majority.

The Court cited no precedential authority for this unprecedented judicial decision except the historic fact that Congress had declared by a resolution of July 21, 1868, that the Fourteenth Amendment had been ratified by the requisite number of states.

Chief Justice Hughes cited this historic fact in an opinion in which only two other Justices concurred.

He added that this decision of the Congress "has been accepted", and suggested that Congress had the unreviewable authority to make it because Congress had power to authorize the Secretary of State to perform the ministerial function of counting the certificates of the states indicating ratification and to promulgate the arithmetic result.

It is certainly not surprising that the congressional decision was "accepted" in 1868. Huge radical majorities in both Houses of Congress had reduced President Andrew Johnson to a state of presidential impotence, and cowed the then Supreme Court itself into complete subservience to their will by threatening to take away the appellate jurisdiction of the Court, and even to abolish the Court itself by constitutional amendment. As a consequence, the Court solemnly adjudged that it did not even have original jurisdiction of "cases . . . in which a state shall be a Party" under clause 2 of section 2 of Article III in April and May, 1867, when Mississippi attempted to secure an injunction to prevent the President from carrying out the reconstruction acts, and Georgia asked the Court to enjoin the military officers from enforcing these acts in that state. (See article on "The United States of America" on page 813 of Volume 22 of the *Encyclopedia Britannica*, Fourteenth Edition.)

Fortunately for the ultimate welfare of our country, the adoption by Congress of the resolution falsely reciting that Ohio and New Jersey had effectually ratified the Fourteenth Amendment was not the only event which occurred in our land on July 21, 1868.

While Congress was proclaiming this untruth, Georgia actually became the twenty-eighth state to ratify the Fourteenth Amendment. By so doing, Georgia rendered the congressional untruth relating to Ohio and New Jersey immaterial, and made ratification of the Fourteenth Amendment an accomplished and acceptable fact.

When all is said, the question of whether a state has ratified or rejected a proposed amendment to the Federal Constitution does not properly come within the scope of the "political-question doctrine" as that doctrine has been enunciated and applied in many Supreme Court cases.

The "political-question doctrine" is based on the separation of governmental powers made by the Constitution itself.

Under the doctrine, the Federal judiciary has no power to make any decision in respect to any question if the power to make the decision is expressly or impliedly committed by the Constitution to some other department or agency of government.

The inapplicability of the "political-question doctrine" to the *Coleman Case* is demonstrated by words used by Chief Justice Hughes himself in that case. He said:

> "In determining whether a question falls within that category, the appropriateness under our system of government of attributing finality to the action of the political departments and also the lack of satisfactory criteria for a judicial determination are dominant considerations." (307 U.S. 433, 454–455)

Both of these considerations were lacking in the *Coleman Case*.

There is not a syllable in Article V or any other provision of the Constitution which intimates in the slightest way that it is appropriate to attribute to a politically-surcharged Congress, which has already declared by a two-thirds vote that a proposed amendment to the Federal Constitution is "necessary", the unreviewable power to make a final decision as to whether the proposed amendment has been ratified in conformity with Article V. On the contrary, Article V and every other provision of the Constitution recoils at the suggestion that the most important question which can arise in our system, i.e., whether our Constitution has been changed by an amendment conforming to Article V, should be left to the final determination of what is essentially a political body which is more concerned with political expediency than with the search for truth. Indeed, Article V and every other provision of the Constitution declare by their words, spirit, and purpose that the decision of this question should be made by the judiciary acting with what Edward Burke described as "the cold neutrality of the impartial judge."

Moreover, there is no basis whatever for claiming a "lack of satisfactory criteria for a judicial determination" of a question of this nature. As a practical matter, the question is susceptible of judicial determination under most circumstances by a simple inspection of certificates issued by the appropriate state officers attesting the action taken by their respective legislatures.

Since the handing down of the *Coleman Case*, the scope of the "political-question doctrine" has been substantially narrowed by *Baker v. Carr*, (1962) 369 U.S. 186, 7 L.Ed.2d 663, 82 S.Ct. 691, where the Court held in repudiation of former decisions that whether a state had unconstitutionally apportioned voting power in the election of state legislators presented a judicial question and not a political question; *Bond v. Floyd*, (1966) 385 U.S. 116, 17 L.Ed.2d 235, 87 S.Ct. 339, where the Court held in substance that whether a state legislature had unconstitutionally deprived a state representative of his seat because of his expressed views presented a judicial question and not a political question; and *Powell v. McCormack*, (1969) 395 U.S. 486, 23 L.Ed.2d 491, 89 S.Ct. 1944, where the Court held in essence that whether the United States House of Representatives had unconstitutionally deprived a Representative of his seat was a judicial question and not a political question.

The Supreme Court expressly declared in *Baker v. Carr* that the relationship between the federal judiciary and the co-ordinate branches of the federal government, and not the federal judiciary's relationship to the states, is what gives rise to the ''political-question doctrine''.

In the light of these decisions and this adjudication, it seems obvious that the Supreme Court will hold if the occasion for its acting in the matter should arise that whether the Equal Rights Amendment has been ratified is a judicial question for the decision of the federal judiciary, and not a political question for the decision of Congress.

Be this as it may, Article V requires that it be decided in accordance with its true meaning, which is that a state may ratify the Amendment if it has previously rejected it, and that a state may rescind or withdraw its ratification if it has previously ratified it.

This April 5, 1977.

2. Charles L. Black, Jr., Sterling Professor of Law, Yale Law School

a. STATEMENT ON LEGALITY OF STATE RESCISSION OF RATIFICATION OF AN AMENDMENT (21 FEBRUARY 1978).

Though I favor the adoption of the Equal Rights Amendment, and would therefore oppose rescission, I am strongly of the opinion that any state may validly rescind its ratification of any proposed amendment, prior to ratification by the requisite three-fourths.

The opposite opinion seems to me to lead to an absurdity. It would be possible, for example, for thirty-seven States to ratify, but for twenty-six of them, say, to decide (perhaps because of some changed condition, or some new insight) to rescind. If those who think rescission or withdrawal is impossible are right, then, if *one more state* ratified, the rest would be stuck with the Amendment, though an actual majority of the States were on record against it as of the time of its going into effect. All kinds of arithmetical variations of this nightmare would be possible, if rescission or withdrawal is ineffective. Theoretically, as you can easily see, it would be possible for an amendment to go into effect which only *one* State—the *last* to ratify— wanted, all the others having tried vainly to rescind. It would be easily possible, if the anti-rescission people are right, to get an amendment not wanted by one-half the States.

These people want to make a sort of one-way lobster-trap, or a silly game of tag, out of a serious constitutional process.

The Fourteenth Amendment "precedent" is thin ice indeed. On the very day (July 21,1868) that Congress (by implication) decided rescission was wrong for Ohio and New Jersey, the Amendment was ratified by Georgia, making up (with the recent Alabama ratification) the requisite three-quarters in any event. This fact was known on the floor of the House of Representatives when the relevant resolution passed; the rescission question was actually moot. Secretary of State Seward, of course, knew this too, when he proclaimed the Amendment on July 28, 1868; the validity of rescission was at that point not relevant. Additional ratifications came through before the Amendment was applied as law.

Coleman v. *Miller* may imply such a question is "political," though the case did not hold on that question. I do not agree with this conclusion. But even if it is right, the "political" classification ought to mean, if it means anything, that one can legitimately draw a line between an ordinary amendment and an amendment which was in effect a part of the treaty of peace ending a civil war.

I don't think the Fourteenth Amendment non-precedent forces us to ignore the absurdity created by the "no-rescission" rule. (I am surprised, moreover, that precedent—even very weak precedent like this—has suddenly become so dominating to so many people not previously distinguished by excessive reverence for precedent.)

It seems that the Fifteenth Amendment "precedent" is no precedent on any possible view, since, despite the New York withdrawal, there were enough States for ratification, and the proclamation by Secretary Fish was wholly routine.

I ought to say, since the question is coming up here and there, that rescission by *referendum* seems to me plainly illegal. Article V names two and only two modes of ratification, and gives Congress the choice between them. Generally speaking, "rescission" of a juristic act must be performed by the person or authority that acted originally; there is no reason for departure from this rule as to the present question.

3. Thomas I. Emerson, Lines Professor Emeritus
of Law, Yale Law School

a. EXCERPT FROM A STATEMENT BEFORE THE GOVERNMENT ADMINISTRATION AND POLICY COMMITTEES OF THE CONNECTICUT GENERAL ASSEMBLY ON THE PROPOSED RESOLUTION TO RESCIND CONNECTICUT'S RATIFICATION OF ERA (16 MARCH 1977).

III

One further question remains. Does a state have the power to withdraw its ratification of the Equal Rights Amendment? Three states—Nebraska, Tennessee, and Idaho—have purported to take such action. And now, of course, Connecticut is being asked to consider rescission.

The legal situation is, I think, reasonably clear. The United States Supreme Court, in the case of *Coleman* v. *Miller*, decided in 1939, held that the question of whether a Constitutional amendment had been properly adopted is not a question for the courts but one which the Constitution has delegated to Congress. It seems most unlikely that the Supreme Court would change its ruling on this point. The final decision, therefore, is one for Congress to make.

In the past Congress has consistently taken the position that a state may not withdraw its ratification of a constitutional amendment. It has adhered to this view in three different instances, the only occasions when the issue has arisen. In connection with the ratification of the Fourteenth Amendment, Ohio and New Jersey attempted to rescind ratification; Congress by resolution nevertheless counted their votes. It should be noted that the votes of these two states were necessary, at the time that action was taken, to make up the required three-quarters vote by which the Fourteenth Amendment was adopted. In the case of the Fifteenth Amendment, New York attempted to withdraw, and in the case of the Nineteenth Amendment (women's suffrage) Tennessee attempted to withdraw. In both instances Congress counted those states as supporting ratification. In the latter two instances, the vote of the rescinding state was not necessary to make up the three-quarters required.

It is thus clear that, unless Congress fails to follow past precedent, rescission is not permissible.

A few experts have argued that Congress should and will change its mind. They have asserted that it is not fair to allow a state to reject a constitutional amendment and then later ratify it, but not allow a state which has ratified to withdraw its approval. There are substantial reasons, however, to support the position which Congress has consistently adopted. As a legal matter, a strong argument can be made that, under the amending process as set forth in the Constitution, a state has only one function, namely to vote ratification or refrain from ratification. If it does vote to ratify its powers are at an end, and there is no further action the state can take. Such a cut-off of legal power is not unknown to the law. If a salesman for the Encyclopedia Britannica comes to your door you may turn him down three times; but if you accept the fourth time you are bound by that action and you cannot rescind.

There are also policy reasons for not allowing rescission. When a constitutional amendment is pending in a state the citizens of that state address their political activities and their votes to that issue. When the amendment is ratified, the voters turn to other matters and the issue no longer is the subject of political attention. To revive the question at a later point is therefore unfair to those who have relied upon the earlier settlement. It also means that the issue may be resolved without benefit of the full political process that the Constitution contemplates.

Under all the circumstances, it would appear that the debate over rescission is an exercise in futility.

IV

In my judgment the Equal Rights Amendment constitutes the focal point—the single most important factor—in the efforts of half of our people to achieve social justice. Failure of this nation to ratify the Equal Rights Amendment would be a moral disaster. Connecticut is proud of its ratification, and we should not budge from that position.

Appendix E

Relevant Legal Cases

1. Chronological Listing

Chisholm v. *Georgia*, 2 U.S. (2 Dall.) 409 (1793).
Hollingsworth v. *Virginia*, 3 U.S. (3 Dall.) 378 (1798).
White v. *Hart*, 80 U.S. (13 Wall.) 646, 649 (1872).
In Re Opinion of the Justices, 118 Me. 544, 549, 107 A. 673, 675 (1919).
Clements v. *Roberts*, 144 Tenn. 129, 230 S.W. 30 (1920).
Dillon v. *Gloss*, 256 U.S. 368, 376 (1920).
Hawke v. *Smith*, 253 U.S. 221, 229 (1920).
U.S. ex rel. Widenmann v. *Colby*, 265 F. 998, 1000 (1920), *aff'd* 257 U.S. 619 (1921).
Leser v. *Garnett*, 258 U.S. 130, 137 (1922).
Chase v. *Billings*, 106 Vt. 149, 155, 170 A.903, 906 (1934).
Coleman v. *Miller*, 146 Kan. 390, 71 P. 2d. 518 (1938); *aff'd.* 307 U.S. 433 (1939).
Wise v. *Chandler*, 270 Ky. 1, 9, 108 S.W. 2d. 1024, 1028, 1031 (1937); *cert. granted* 303 U.S. 634 (1938); *aff'd. on other grounds*, 307 U.S. 474 (1939).
U.S. v. *Gugel*, 119 F. Supp. 897 (E.D. Ky. 1954).
Baker v. *Carr*, 369 U.S. 186 (1962).
Jackman v. *Bodine*, 43 N.J. 453, 205 A. 2d. 713, 723 (1964).
Reynolds v. *Sims*, 377 U.S. 533 (1964).
Moore v. *Moore*, 229 F. Supp. 435, 438 (S.D. Ala. 1964).
Butterworth v. *Dempsey*, 237 F. Supp. 302, 308 (D. Conn. 1965).
Buchanan v. *Rhodes*, 249 F. Supp. 860, 864 (S.D. Ohio 1966).
Maryland Petition Committee v. *Johnson*, 265 F. Supp. 823 (D. Md. 1967).
Powell v. *McCormack*, 395 U.S. 486 (1969).
Sierra Club v. *Morton*, 405 U.S. 727 (1972).
Walker v. *Dunn*, 498 S.W. 2d. 102 (Tenn. 1972).
Hatch v. *Murray*, 165 Mt. 94, 526 P. 2d. 1369 (1974).
Vincent v. *Schlesinger*, 388 F. Supp. 370, 373 (D.D.C. 1975).
Askew v. *Meier*, 231 N.W. 2d. 821 (N.D. 1975).
Dyer v. *Blair*, 390 F. Supp. 1291, 1306 (S.D. Ill. 1975).

2. Excerpts from *Hawke* v. *Smith*, 253 U.S. 221 (1920)

[Action to enjoin submission of the Eighteenth Amendment to a referendum pursuant to the Ohio constitution. Mr. Justice Day delivered the opinion of the court.]

The question for our consideration is: Whether the provision of the Ohio constitution, adopted at the general election, November, 1918, extending the referendum to the ratification by the General Assembly of proposed amendments to the Federal Constitution is in conflict with Article V of the Constitution of the United States. The Amendment of 1918 provides: "The people also reserve to themselves the legislative power of the referendum on the action of the general assembly ratifying any proposed amendment to the constitution of the United States." [Quotes Article V]. . . .

The framers of the Constitution realized that it might in the progress of time and the development of new conditions require changes, and they intended to provide an orderly manner in which these could be accomplished; to that end they adopted the Fifth Article. . . .

The Fifth Article is a grant of authority by the people to Congress. The determination of the method of ratification is the exercise of a national power specifically granted by the Constitution; that power is conferred upon Congress, and is limited to two methods, by action of the legislatures of three-fourths of the States, or conventions in a like number of States. *Dodge* v. *Woolsey*, 18 How. 331, 348. The framers of the Constitution might have adopted a different method. Ratification might have been left to a vote of the people, or to some authority of government other than that selected. The language of the article is plain, and admits of no doubt in its interpretation. It is not the function of courts or legislative bodies, national or state, to alter the method which the Constitution has fixed. . . .

The only question really for determination is: What did the framers of the Constitution mean in requiring ratification by "*Legislatures*"? That was not a term of uncertain meaning when incorporated into the Constitution. What it meant when adopted it still means for the purpose of interpretation. A Legislature was then the representative body which made the laws of the people. The term is often used in the Constitution with this evident meaning. . . .

There can be no question that the framers of the Constitution clearly understood and carefully used the terms in which that instrument referred to the action of the legislatures of the States. When they intended that direct action by the people should be had they were no less accurate in the use of apt phraseology to carry out such purpose. The members of the House of Representatives were required to be chosen by the people of the several States. Article I, § 2. . . .

The argument to support the power of the State to require the approval by the people of the State of the ratification of amendments to the Federal Constitution through the medium of a referendum rests upon the proposition that the Federal Constitution requires ratification by the legislative action of the States through the medium provided at the time of the proposed approval of an amendment. This argument is fallacious in this—ratification by a State of a constitutional amendment is not an act of legislation within the proper sense of the word. It is but the expression of the assent of the State to a proposed amendment. . . .

It is true that the power to legislate in the enactment of the laws of a State is derived from the people of the State. But the power to ratify a proposed amendment to the Federal Constitution has its source in the Federal Constitution. The act of ratification by the State derives its authority from the Federal Constitution to which the State and its people have alike assented. . . .

It follows that the court erred in holding that the State had authority to require the submission of the ratification to a referendum under the state constitution, and its judgment is reversed and the cause remanded for further proceedings not inconsistent with this opinion.

Reversed.

3. Excerpts from *U.S. ex rel Widenmann* v. *Colby,* 265 F. 998 (1920); *aff'd* 257 U.S. 619 (1921)

[Smyth, Chief Justice. Action against the secretary of state for a mandamus commanding him to cancel the proclamation declaring the Eighteenth Amendment validly ratified.]

Section 205 of the Revised Statutes of the United States reads: "Whenever official notice is received at the Department of State that any amendment proposed to the Constitution of the United States has been adopted according to the provisions of the Constitution, the Secretary of State shall forthwith cause the amendment to be published in the newspapers authorized to promulgate the laws, with his certificate, specifying the States by which the same may have been adopted, and that the same has become valid, to all intents and purposes, as a part of the Constitution of the United States."

It will be observed that by this section [it] was the duty of the Acting Secretary of State, upon receiving official notice from three-fourths of the several states (Constitution, art. 5) that the proposed amendment had been adopted, to issue his proclamation. He was not required, or authorized, to investigate and determine whether or not the notices stated the truth. To accept them as doing so, if in due form, was his duty. As soon as he had received the notices from 36 of the states that the amendment had been adopted, he was obliged, under the statute, to put forth his proclamation. No discretion was lodged in him. The act required was purely ministerial. . . . [T]he Acting Secretary had no authority to examine into that matter, to look behind the notices. From these considerations it follows that the Acting Secretary, instead of failing to perform a duty imposed upon him by statute, the performance of which should be coerced by mandamus, performed a duty enjoined upon him by statute in issuing the proclamation in question. Under those circumstances there is no basis for the relief sought by the petitioner. . . .

Moreover, even if the proclamation was canceled by order of this court, it would not affect the validity of the amendment. Its validity does not depend in any wise upon the proclamation. It is the approval of the requisite number of states, not the proclamation, that gives vitality to the amendment and makes it a part of the supreme law of the land. . . .

Perceiving no error in the action of the trial court, we affirm the judgment with costs.

4. Excerpts from *Dillon* v. *Gloss,* 256 U.S. 368 (1920)

[Appeal from a denial of habeas corpus for a prisoner convicted of violating the National Prohibition Act. Petitioner claimed that the Eighteenth Amendment, and hence the act pursuant to it, were invalid. Mr. Justice Van Devanter delivered the opinion of the court.]

The power to amend the Constitution and the mode of exerting it are dealt with in Article V. . . .

It will be seen that this article says nothing about the time within which ratification may be had—neither that it shall be unlimited nor that it shall be fixed by Congress. What then is the reasonable inference or implication? Is it that ratification may be had at any time, as within a few years, a century or even a longer period; or that it must be had within some reasonable period which Congress is left free to define? Neither the debates in the federal convention which framed the Constitution nor those in the state conventions which ratified it shed any light on the question.

The proposal for the Eighteenth Amendment is the first in which a definite period for ratification was fixed [footnote deleted]. Theretofore twenty-one amendments had been proposed by Congress and seventeen of these had been ratified by the legislatures of three-fourths of the States,—some within a single year after their proposal and all within four years. . . .

. . . Whether an amendment proposed without fixing any time for ratification, and which after favorable action in less than the required number of States had lain dormant for many years, could be resurrected and its ratification completed had been mooted on several occasions, but was still an open question.

These were the circumstances in the light of which Congress in proposing the Eighteenth Amendment fixed seven years as the period for ratification. Whether this could be done was questioned at the time and debated at length, but the prevailing view in both houses was that some limitation was intended and that seven years was a reasonable period [footnote deleted].

That the Constitution contains no express provision on the subject is not in itself controlling; for with the Constitution, as with a statute or other written instrument, what is reasonably implied is as much a part of it as what is expressed [footnote deleted]. An examination of Article V discloses that it is intended to invest Congress with a wide range of power in proposing amendments. . . . Thus the people of the United States, by whom the Constitution was ordained and established, have made it a condition to amending that instrument that the amendment be submitted to representative assemblies in the several States and be ratified in three-fourths of them. The plain meaning of this is (a) that all amendments must have the sanction of the people of the United States, the original fountain of power, acting through representative assemblies, and (b) that ratification by these assemblies in three-fourths of the States shall be taken as a decisive expression of the people's will and be binding on all [footnote deleted].

We do not find anything in the Article which suggests that an amendment once proposed is to be open to ratification for all time, or that ratification in some of the States may be separated from that in others by many years and yet be effective. We do find that which strongly suggests the contrary. First, proposal and ratification are not treated as unrelated acts but as succeeding steps in a single endeavor, the natural inference being that they are not to be widely separated in time. Secondly, . . . when proposed they are to be considered and disposed of presently. Thirdly, . . . there is a fair implication that it must be sufficiently contemporaneous in that number of States to reflect the will of the people in all sections at relatively the same period, which of course ratification scattered through a long series of years would not do. These considerations and the general purport and spirit of the Article lead to the conclusion expressed by Judge Jameson [footnote deleted] "that an alteration of the Constitution proposed today has relation to the sentiment and the felt needs of today, and that, if not ratified early while that sentiment may fairly be supposed to exist, it ought to be regarded as waived, and not again to be voted upon, unless a second time proposed by Congress.'' That this is the better conclusion becomes even more manifest when what is comprehended in the other view is considered; for, according to it, four amendments proposed long ago—two in 1789, one in 1810 and one in 1861—are still pending and in a situation where their ratification in some of the States many years since by representatives of generations now largely forgotten may be effectively supplemented in enough more States to make three-fourths by representatives of the present or some future generation. To that view few would be able to subscribe, and in our opinion it is quite untenable. We conclude that the fair inference or implication from Article V is that the ratification must be within some reasonable time after the proposal.

Of the power of Congress, keeping within reasonable limits, to fix a definite period for the ratification we entertain no doubt. As a rule the Constitution speaks in general terms, leaving Congress to deal with subsidiary matters of detail as the public interests and changing conditions may require [footnote deleted]; and Article V is no exception to the rule. Whether a definite period for ratification shall be fixed so that all may know what it is and speculation on what is a reasonable time may be avoided, is, in our opinion, a matter of detail which Congress may determine as an incident of its power to designate the mode of ratification. It is not questioned that seven years, the period fixed in this instance, was reasonable, if power existed to fix a definite time; nor could it well be questioned considering the periods within which prior amendments were ratified. . . .

Final order affirmed.

5. Excerpts from *Leser* v. *Garnett*, 258 U.S. 130 (1922)

[Action to strike the names of two women from the Baltimore voters' list because the Maryland constitution limited suffrage to men. Maryland did not ratify the Nineteenth Amendment granting women the right to vote. Mr. Justice Brandeis delivered the opinion of the court.]

. . . This Amendment is in character and phraseology precisely similar to the Fifteenth. For each the same method of adoption was pursued. One cannot be valid and the other invalid. That the Fifteenth is valid, although rejected by six States including Maryland, has been recognized and acted on for half a century. . . . The suggestion that the Fifteenth was incorporated in the Constitution, not in accordance with law, but practically as a war measure which has been validated by acquiescence, cannot be entertained.

The second contention is that in the constitutions of several of the thirty-six States named in the proclamation of the Secretary of State there are provisions which render inoperative the alleged ratifications by their legislatures. The argument is that by reason of these specific provisions the legislatures were without power to ratify. But the function of a state legislature in ratifying a proposed amendment to the Federal Constitution, like the function of Congress in proposing the amendment, is a federal function derived from the Federal Constitution; and it transcends any limitations sought to be imposed by the people of a State. . . .

The remaining contention is that the ratifying resolutions of Tennessee and of West Virginia are inoperative, because adopted in violation of the rules of legislative procedure prevailing in the respective States. The question raised may have been rendered immaterial by the fact that since the proclamation the legislatures of two other States—Connecticut and Vermont—have adopted resolutions of ratification. But a broader answer should be given to the contention. The proclamation by the Secretary certified that from official documents on file in the Department of State it appeared that the proposed Amendment was ratified by the legislatures of thirty-six States, and that it "has become valid to all intents and purposes as a part of the Constitution of the United States." As the legislatures of Tennessee and of West Virginia had power to adopt the resolutions of ratification, official notice to the Secretary, duly authenticated, that they had done so was conclusive upon him, and, being certified to by his proclamation, is conclusive upon the courts. . . .

Affirmed.

6. *Coleman* v. *Miller*, 307 U.S. 433 (1939)

Because of the controversy surrounding the meaning of the four opinions in the decision, they are reprinted here in their entirety. Original footnotes follow the texts. Although writers often refer to three opinions, technically there are four. Justice Frankfurter joined in Justice Black's concurring opinion, but he also wrote a second concurring opinion.

a. OPINION OF THE COURT BY MR. CHIEF JUSTICE HUGHES, ANNOUNCED BY MR. JUSTICE STONE.

In June, 1924, the Congress proposed an amendment to the Constitution, known as the Child Labor Amendment.[1] In January, 1925, the Legislature of Kansas adopted a resolution rejecting the proposed amendment and a certified copy of the resolution was sent to the Secretary of State of the United States. In January, 1937, a resolution known as "Senate Concurrent Resolution No. 3" was introduced in the Senate of Kansas ratifying the proposed amendment. There were forty senators. When the resolution came up for consideration, twenty senators voted in favor of its adoption and twenty voted against it. The Lieutenant Governor, the presiding officer of the Senate, then cast his vote in favor of the resolution. The resolution was later adopted by the House of Representatives on the vote of a majority of its members.

This original proceeding in mandamus was then brought in the Supreme Court of Kansas by twenty-one members of the Senate, including the twenty senators who had voted against the resolution, and three members of the House of Representatives, to compel the Secretary of the Senate to erase an endorsement on the resolution to the effect that it had been adopted by the Senate and to endorse thereon the words "was not passed," and to restrain the officers of the Senate and House of Representatives from signing the resolution and the Secretary of State of Kansas from authenticating it and delivering it to the Governor. The petition challenged the right of the Lieutenant Governor to cast the deciding vote in the Senate. The petition also set forth the prior rejection of the proposed amendment and alleged that in the period from June, 1924, to March, 1927, the amendment had been rejected by both houses of the legislatures of twenty-six States, and had been ratified in only five States, and that by reason of that rejection and the failure of ratification within a reasonable time the proposed amendment had lost its vitality.

An alternative writ was issued. Later the Senate passed a resolution directing the Attorney General to enter the appearance of the State and to represent the State as its interests might appear. Answers were filed on behalf of the defendants other than the State and plaintiffs made their reply.

The Supreme Court found no dispute as to the facts. The court entertained the action and held that the Lieutenant Governor was authorized to cast the deciding vote, that the proposed amendment retained its original vitality, and that the resolution "having duly passed the house of representatives and the senate, the act of ratification of the proposed amendment by the legislature of Kansas was final and complete." The writ of mandamus was accordingly denied. 146 Kan. 390; 71 P. 2d 518. This Court granted certiorari. 303 U.S. 632.

First. The jurisdiction of this Court. Our authority to issue the writ of certiorari is challenged upon the ground that petitioners have no standing to seek to have the judgment of the state court reviewed, and hence it is urged that the writ of certiorari should be dismissed. We are unable to accept that view.

The state court held that it had jurisdiction; that "the right of the parties to maintain the action is beyond question."[2] The state court thus determined in substance that members of the legislature had standing to seek, and the court had jurisdiction to grant, mandamus to compel a proper record of legislative action. Had the questions been solely state questions, the matter would have ended there. But the questions raised in the instant case arose under the Federal Constitution and these questions were entertained and decided by the state court. They arose under Article V of the Constitution which alone conferred the power to amend and determined the manner in which that power could be exercised. *Hawke* v. *Smith (No. 1)*, 253 U.S. 221, 227; *Leser* v. *Garnett*, 258 U.S. 130, 137. Whether any or all of the questions thus raised and decided are deemed to be justiciable or political, they are exclusively federal questions and not state questions.

We find the cases cited in support of the contention, that petitioners lack an adequate interest to invoke our jurisdiction to review, to be inapplicable.[3] Here, the plaintiffs include twenty senators, whose votes against ratification have been overridden and virtually held for naught although if they are right in their contentions their votes would have been sufficient to defeat ratification. We think that these senators have a plain, direct and adequate interest in maintaining the effectiveness of their votes. Petitioners come directly within the provisions of the statute governing our appellate jurisdiction. They have set up and claimed a right and privilege under the Constitution of the United States to have their votes given effect and the state court has denied that right and privilege. As the validity of a state statute was not assailed, the remedy by appeal was not available (Jud. Code, § 237 (a); 28 U.S. C. 344 (a)) and the appropriate remedy was by writ of certiorari which we granted. Jud. Code., § 237 (b); 28 U.S. C. 344 (b).

The contention to the contrary is answered by our decisions in *Hawke* v. *Smith, supra*, and *Leser* v. *Garnett, supra*. In *Hawke* v. *Smith*, the plaintiff in error, suing as a "citizen and elector of the State of Ohio, and as a taxpayer and elector of the County of Hamilton," on behalf of himself and others similarly situated, filed a petition for an injunction in the state court to restrain the Secretary of State from spending the public money in preparing and printing ballots for submission of a referendum to the electors on the question of the ratification of the Eighteenth Amendment to the Federal Constitution. A demurrer to the petition was sustained in the lower court and its judgment was affirmed by the intermediate appellate court and the Supreme Court of the State. This Court entertained jurisdiction and, holding that the state court had erred in deciding that the State had authority to require the submission of the ratification to a referendum, reversed the judgment.

In *Leser* v. *Garnett*, qualified voters in the State of Maryland brought suit in the state court to have the names of certain women stricken from the list of qualified voters on the ground that the constitution of Maryland limited suffrage to men and that the Nineteenth Amendment to the Federal Constitution has not been validly ratified. The state court took jurisdiction and the Court of Appeals of the State affirmed the judgment dismissing the petition. We granted certiorari. On the question of our jurisdiction we said:

> The petitioners contended, on several grounds, that the Amendment had not become part of the Federal Constitution. The trial court overruled the contentions and dismissed the petition. Its judgment was affirmed by the Court of Appeals of the State, 139 Md. 46; and the case comes here on writ of error. That writ must be dismissed; but the petition for a writ of certiorari, also duly filed, is granted. The laws of Maryland authorized such a suit by a qualified voter against the Board of Registry. Whether the Nineteenth Amendment has become part of the Federal Constitution is the question presented for decision.

And holding that the official notice to the Secretary of State, duly authenticated, of the action of the legislatures of the States, whose alleged ratifications were assailed, was conclusive upon the Secretary of State and that his proclamation accordingly of ratification was conclusive upon the courts, we affirmed the judgment of the state court.

That the question of our jurisdiction in *Leser* v. *Garnett* was decided upon deliberate consideration is sufficiently shown by the fact that there was a motion to dismiss the writ of error for the want of jurisdiction and opposition to the grant of certiorari. The decision is the more striking because on the same day, in an opinion immediately preceding which was prepared for the Court by the same Justice,[4] jurisdiction had been denied to a federal court (the Supreme Court of the District of Columbia) of a suit by citizens of the United States, taxpayers and members of a voluntary association organized to support the Constitution, in which it was sought to have the Nineteenth Amendment declared unconstitutional and to enjoin the Secretary of State from proclaiming its ratification and the Attorney General from taking steps to enforce it. *Fairchild* v. *Hughes*, 258 U.S. 126. The Court held that the plaintiffs' alleged interest in the question submitted was not such as to afford a basis for the proceeding; that the plaintiffs had only the right possessed by every citizen "to require that the Government be administered according to law and that the public moneys be not wasted" and that this general right did not entitle a private citizen to bring such a suit as the one in question in the federal courts.[5] It would be difficult to imagine a situation in which the adequacy of the petitioners' interest to invoke our appellate jurisdiction in *Leser* v. *Garnett* could have been more sharply presented.

The effort to distinguish that case on the ground that the plaintiffs were qualified voters in Maryland, and hence could complain of the admission to the registry of those alleged not to be qualified, is futile. The interest of the plaintiffs in *Leser* v. *Garnett* as merely qualified voters at general elections is certainly much less impressive than the interest of the twenty senators in the instant case. This is not a mere intra-parliamentary controversy but the question relates to legislative action deriving its force solely from the provisions of the Federal Constitution, and the twenty senators were not only qualified to vote on the question of ratification but their votes, if the Lieutenant Governor were excluded as not being a part of the legislature for that purpose, would have been decisive in defeating the ratifying resolution.

We are of the opinion that *Hawke* v. *Smith* and *Leser* v. *Garnett* are controlling authorities, but in view of the wide range the discussion has taken we may refer to some other instances in which the question of what constitutes a sufficient interest to enable one to invoke our appellate jurisdiction has been involved. The principle that the applicant must show a legal interest in the controversy has been maintained. It has been applied repeatedly in cases where municipal corporations have challenged state legislation affecting their alleged rights and obligations. Being but creatures of the State, municipal corporations have no standing to invoke the contract clause or the provisions of the Fourteenth Amendment of the Constitution in opposition to the will of their creator.[6] But there has been recognition of the legitimate interest of public officials and administrative commissions, federal and state, to resist the endeavor to prevent the enforcement of statutes in relation to which they have official duties. Under the Urgent Deficiencies Act,[7] the Interstate Commerce Commission, and commissions representing interested States which have intervened, are entitled as ''aggrieved parties'' to an appeal to this Court from a decree setting aside an order of the Interstate Commerce Commission, though the United States refuses to join in the appeal. *Interstate Commerce Comm'n* v. *Oregon-Washington R. & N. Co*, 288 U. S. 14. So, this Court may grant certiorari, on the application of the Federal Trade Commission, to review decisions setting aside its orders.[8] *Federal Trade Comm'n* v. *Curtis Publishing Co.*, 260 U. S. 568. Analogous provisions authorize certiorari to review decisions against the National Labor Relations Board.[9] *National Labor Relations Board* v. *Jones & Laughlin Corp.*, 301 U. S. 1. Under § 266 of the Judicial Code (28 U. S. C. 380), where an injunction is sought to restrain the enforcement of a statute of a State or an order of its administrative board or commission, upon the ground of invalidity under the Federal Constitution, the right of direct appeal to this Court from the decree of the required three judges is accorded whether the injunction be granted or denied. Hence, in case the injunction is granted, the state board is entitled to appeal. See, for example, *South Carolina Highway Dept.* v. *Barnwell Brothers*, 303 U. S. 177.

The question of our authority to grant certiorari, on the application of state officers, to review decisions of state courts declaring state statutes, which these officers seek to enforce, to be repugnant to the Federal Constitution, has been carefully considered and our jurisdiction in that class of cases has been sustained. The original Judiciary Act of 1789 provided in § 25[10] for the review by this Court of a judgment of a state court "where is drawn in question the validity of a statute of, or an authority exercised under any State, on the ground of their being repugnant to the constitution, treaties or laws of the United States, and the decision is in favour of such their validity"; that is, where the claim of federal right had been *denied.* By the Act of December 23, 1914,[11] it was provided that this Court may review on certiorari decisions of state courts *sustaining* a federal right. The present statute governing our jurisdiction on certiorari contains the corresponding provision that this Court may exercise that jurisdiction "as well where the federal claim is sustained as where it is denied." Jud. Code, § 237 (b); 28 U.S.C. 344 (b). The plain purpose was to provide an opportunity, deemed to be important and appropriate, for the review of the decisions of state courts on constitutional questions however the state court might decide them. Accordingly where the claim of a complainant that a state officer be restrained from enforcing a state statute because of constitutional invalidity is sustained by the state court, the statute enables the state officer to seek a reversal by this Court of that decision.

In *Blodgett* v. *Silberman*, 277 U.S. 1, 7, the Court granted certiorari on the application of the State Tax Commissioner of Connecticut who sought review of the decision of the Supreme Court of Errors of the State so far as it denied the right created by its statute to tax the transfer of certain securities, which had been placed for safekeeping in New York, on the ground that they were not within the taxing jurisdiction of Connecticut. Entertaining jurisdiction, this Court reversed the judgment in that respect. *Id.*, p. 18.

The question received most careful consideration in the case of *Boynton* v. *Hutchinson Gas Co.*, 291 U.S. 656, where the Supreme Court of Kansas had held a state statute to be repugnant to the Federal Constitution, and the Attorney General of the State applied for certiorari. His application was opposed upon the ground that he had merely an official interest in the controversy and the decisions were invoked upon which the Government relies in challenging our jurisdiction in the instant case.[12] Because of its importance, and contrary to our usual practice, the Court directed oral argument on the question whether certiorari should be granted, and after that argument, upon mature deliberation, granted the writ. The writ was subsequently dismissed but only because of a failure of the record to show service of summons and severance upon the appellees in the state court who were not parties to the proceedings here. 292 U.S. 601. This decision with respect to the scope of our jurisdiction has been followed in later cases. In *Morehead* v. *New York ex rel. Tipaldo*, 298 U.S. 587, we granted certiorari on an application by the warden of a city prison to review the decision of the Court of Appeals of the State on *habeas corpus*, ruling that the minimum wage law of the State violated the Federal Constitution. This Court decided the case on the merits. In *Kelly* v. *Washington ex rel. Foss Co.*, 302 U.S. 1, we granted certiorari, on the application of the state authorities charged with the enforcement of the state law relating to the inspection and regulation of vessels, to review the decision of the state court holding the statute invalid in its application to navigable waters. We concluded that the state act had a permissible field of operation and the decision of the state court in holding the statute completely unenforceable in deference to federal law was reversed.

This class of cases in which we have exercised our appellate jurisdiction on the application of state officers may be said to recognize that they have an adequate interest in the controversy by reason of their duty to enforce the state statutes the validity of which has been drawn in question. In none of these cases could it be said that the state officers invoking our jurisdiction were sustaining any "private damage."

While one who asserts the mere right of a citizen and taxpayer of the United States to complain of the alleged invalid outlay of public moneys has no standing to invoke the jurisdiction of the federal courts (*Frothingham* v. *Mellon*, 262 U.S. 447, 480, 486, 487), the Court has sustained the more immediate and substantial right of a resident taxpayer to invoke the interposition of a court of equity to enjoin an illegal use of moneys by a municipal corporation. *Crampton* v. *Zabriskie*, 101 U.S. 601, 609; *Frothingham* v. *Mellon, supra.* In *Heim* v. *McCall*, 239 U.S. 175, we took jurisdiction on a writ of error sued out by a property owner and taxpayer, who had been given standing in the state court, for the purpose of reviewing its decision sustaining the validity under the Federal Constitution, of a state statute as applied to contracts for the construction of public works in the City of New York, the enforcement of which was alleged to involve irreparable loss to the city and hence to be inimical to the interests of the taxpayer.

In *Smiley* v. *Holm*, 285 U.S. 355, we granted certiorari on the application of one who was an "elector," as well as a "citizen" and "taxpayer," and who assailed under the Federal Constitution a state statute establishing congressional districts. Passing upon the merits we held that the function of a state legislature in prescribing the time, place and manner of holding elections for representatives in Congress under Article I, § 4, was a law-making function in which the veto power of the state governor participates, if under the state constitution the governor has that power in the course of the making of state laws, and accordingly reversed the judgment of the state court. We took jurisdiction on certiorari in a similar case from New York where the petitioners were "citizens and voters of the State" who had sought a mandamus to compel the Secretary of State of New York to certify that representatives in Congress were to be elected in the congressional districts as defined by a concurrent resolution of the Senate and Assembly of the legislature. There the state court, construing the provision of the Federal Constitution as contemplating the exercise of the law-making power, had sustained the defense that the concurrent resolution was ineffective as it had not been submitted to the Governor for approval, and refused the writ of mandamus. We affirmed the judgment. *Koenig* v. *Flynn*, 285 U.S. 375.

In the light of this course of decisions, we find no departure from principle in recognizing in the instant case that at least the twenty senators whose votes, if their contention were sustained, would have been sufficient to defeat the resolution ratifying the proposed constitutional amendment, have an interest in the controversy which, treated by the state court as a basis for entertaining and deciding the federal questions, is sufficient to give the Court jurisdiction to review that decision.

Second. The participation of the Lieutenant Governor. Petitioners contend that, in the light of the powers and duties of the Lieutenant Governor and his relation to the Senate under the state constitution, as construed by the supreme court of the state, the Lieutenant Governor was not a part of the "legislature" so that under Article V of the Federal Constitution, he could be permitted to have a deciding vote on the ratification of the proposed amendment, when the senate was equally divided.

Whether this contention presents a justiciable controversy, or a question which is political in its nature and hence not justiciable, is a question upon which the Court is equally divided and therefore the Court expresses no opinion upon that point.

Third. The effect of the previous rejection of the amendment and of the lapse of time since its submission.

1. The state court adopted the view expressed by text-writers that a state legislature which has rejected an amendment proposed by the Congress may later ratify.[13] The argument in support of that view is that Article V says nothing of rejection but speaks only of ratification and provides that a proposed amendment shall be valid as part of the Constitution when ratified by three-fourths of the States; that the power to ratify is thus conferred upon the State by the Constitution and, as a ratifying power, persists despite a previous rejection. The opposing view proceeds on an assumption that if ratification by "Conventions" were prescribed by the Congress, a convention could not reject and, having adjourned *sine die*, be reassembled and ratify. It is also premised, in accordance with views expressed by text-writers,[14] that ratification if once given cannot afterwards be rescinded and the amendment rejected, and it is urged that the same effect in the exhaustion of the State's power to act should be ascribed to rejection; that a State can act "but once, either by convention or through its legislature."

Historic instances are cited. In 1865, the Thirteenth Amendment was rejected by the legislature of New Jersey which subsequently ratified it, but the question did not become important as ratification by the requisite number of States had already been proclaimed.[15] The question did arise in connection with the adoption of the Fourteenth Amendment. The legislatures of Georgia, North Carolina and South Carolina had rejected the amendment in November and December, 1866.[16] New governments were erected in those States (and in others) under the direction of Congress.[17] The new legislatures ratified the amendment, that of North Carolina on July 4, 1868, that of South Carolina on July 9, 1868, and that of Georgia on July 21, 1868.[18] Ohio and New Jersey first ratified and then passed resolutions withdrawing their consent.[19] As there were then thirty-seven States, twenty-eight were needed to constitute the requisite three-fourths. On July 9, 1868, the Congress adopted a resolution requesting the Secretary of State to communicate "a list of the States of the Union whose legislatures have ratified the fourteenth article of amendment,"[20] and in Secretary Seward's report attention was called to the action of Ohio and New Jersey.[21] On July 20th Secretary Seward issued a proclamation reciting the ratification by twenty-eight States, including North Carolina, South Carolina, Ohio and New Jersey, and stating that it appeared that Ohio and New Jersey had since passed resolutions withdrawing their consent and that "it is deemed a matter of doubt and uncertainty whether such resolutions are not irregular, invalid and therefore ineffectual." The Secretary certified that if the ratifying resolutions of Ohio and New Jersey were still in full force and effect, notwithstanding the attempted withdrawal, the amendment had become a part of the Constitution.[22] On the following day the Congress adopted a concurrent resolution which, reciting that three-fourths of the States having ratified (the list including North Carolina, South Carolina, Ohio and New Jersey),[23] declared the Fourteenth Amendment to be a part of the Constitution and that it should be duly promulgated as such by the Secretary of State. Accordingly, Secretary Seward, on July 28th, issued his proclamation embracing the States mentioned in the congressional resolution and adding Georgia.[24]

Thus the political departments of the Government dealt with the effect both of previous rejection and of attempted withdrawal and determined that both were ineffectual in the presence of an actual ratification.[25] While there were special circumstances, because of the action of the Congress in relation to the governments of the rejecting States (North Carolina, South Carolina and Georgia), these circumstances were not recited in proclaiming ratification and the previous action taken in these States was set forth in the proclamation as actual previous rejections by the respective legislatures. This decision by the political departments of the Government as to the validity of the adoption of the Fourteenth Amendment has been accepted.

We think that in accordance with this historic precedent the question of the efficacy of ratifications by state legislatures, in the light of previous rejection or attempted withdrawal, should be regarded as a political question pertaining to the political departments, with the ultimate authority in the Congress in the exercise of its control over the promulgation of the adoption of the amendment.

The precise question as now raised is whether, when the legislature of the State, as we have found, has actually ratified the proposed amendment, the Court should restrain the state officers from certifying the ratification to the Secretary of State, because of an earlier rejection, and thus prevent the question from coming before the political departments. We find no basis in either Constitution or statute for such judicial action. Article V, speaking solely of ratification, contains no provision as to rejection.[26] Nor has the Congress enacted a statute relating to rejections. The statutory provision with respect to constitutional amendments is as follows:

"Whenever official notice is received at the Department of State that any amendment proposed to the Constitution of the United States has been adopted, according to the provisions of the Constitution, the Secretary of State shall forthwith cause the amendment to be published, with his certificate, specifying the States by which the same may have been adopted, and that the same has become valid, to all intents and purposes, as a part of the Constitution of the United States.''[27]

The statute presupposes official notice to the Secretary of State when a state legislature has adopted a resolution of ratification. We see no warrant for judicial interference with the performance of that duty. See *Leser* v. *Garnett, supra*, p. 137.

2. The more serious question is whether the proposal by the Congress of the amendment had lost its vitality through lapse of time and hence it could not be ratified by the Kansas legislature in 1937. The argument of petitioners stresses the fact that nearly thirteen years elapsed between the proposal in 1924 and the ratification in question. It is said that when the amendment was proposed there was a definitely adverse popular sentiment and that at the end of 1925 there had been rejection by both houses of the legislatures of sixteen States and ratification by only four States, and that it was not until about 1933 that an aggressive campaign was started in favor of the amendment. In reply, it is urged that Congress did not fix a limit of time for ratification and that an unreasonably long time had not elapsed since the submission; that the conditions which gave rise to the amendment had not been eliminated; that the prevalence of child labor, the diversity of state laws and the disparity in their administration, with the resulting competitive inequalities, continued to exist. Reference is also made to the fact that a number of the States have treated the amendment as still pending and that in the proceedings of the national government there have been indications of the same view.[28] It is said that there were fourteen ratifications in 1933, four in 1935, one in 1936, and three in 1937.

We have held that the Congress in proposing an amendment may fix a reasonable time for ratification. *Dillon* v. *Gloss*, 256 U.S. 368. There we sustained the action of the Congress in providing in the proposed Eighteenth Amendment that it should be inoperative unless ratified within seven years.[29] No limitation of time for ratification is provided in the instant case either in the proposed amendment or in the resolution of submission. But petitioners contend that, in the absence of a limitation by the Congress, the Court can and should decide what is a reasonable period within which ratification may be had. We are unable to agree with that contention.

It is true that in *Dillon* v. *Gloss* the Court said that nothing was found in Article V which suggested that an amendment once proposed was to be open to ratification for all time, or that ratification in some States might be separated from that in others by many years and yet be effective; that there was a strong suggestion to the contrary in that proposal and ratification were but succeeding steps in a single endeavor; that as amendments were deemed to be prompted by necessity, they should be considered and disposed of presently; and that there is a fair implication that ratification must be sufficiently contemporaneous in the required number of States to reflect the will of the people in all sections at relatively the same period; and hence that ratification must be within some reasonable time after the proposal. These considerations were cogent reasons for the decision in *Dillon* v. *Gloss* that the Congress had the power to fix a reasonable time for ratification. But it does not follow that, whenever Congress has not exercised that power, the Court should take upon itself the responsibility of deciding what constitutes a reasonable time and determine accordingly the validity of ratifications. That question was not involved in *Dillon* v. *Gloss* and, in accordance with familiar principle, what was there said must be read in the light of the point decided.

　　3. Where are to be found the criteria for such a judicial determination? None are to be found in Constitution or statute. In their endeavor to answer this question petitioners' counsel have suggested that at least two years should be allowed; that six years would not seem to be unreasonably long; that seven years had been used by the Congress as a reasonable period; that one year, six months and thirteen days was the average time used in passing upon amendments which have been ratified since the first ten amendments; that three years, six months and twenty-five days has been the longest time used in ratifying. To this list of variables, counsel add that "the nature and extent of publicity and the activity of the public and of the legislatures of the several States in relation to any particular proposal should be taken into consideration." That statement is pertinent, but there are additional matters to be examined and weighed. When a proposed amendment springs from a conception of economic needs, it would be necessary, in determining whether a reasonable time had elapsed since its submission, to consider the economic conditions prevailing in the country, whether these had so far changed since the submission as to make the proposal no longer responsive to the conception which inspired it or whether conditions were such as to intensify the feeling of need and the appropriateness of the proposed remedial action. In short, the question of a reasonable time in many cases would involve, as in this case it does involve, an appraisal of a great variety of relevant conditions, political, social and economic, which can hardly be said to be within the appropriate range of evidence receivable

in a court of justice and as to which it would be an extravagant extension of judicial authority to assert judicial notice as the basis of deciding a controversy with respect to the validity of an amendment actually ratified. On the other hand, these conditions are appropriate for the consideration of the political departments of the Government. The questions they involve are essentially political and not justiciable. They can be decided by the Congress with the full knowledge and appreciation ascribed to the national legislature of the political, social and economic conditions which have prevailed during the period since the submission of the amendment.

Our decision that the Congress has the power under Article V to fix a reasonable limit of time for ratification in proposing an amendment proceeds upon the assumption that the question, what is a reasonable time, lies within the congressional province. If it be deemed that such a question is an open one when the limit has not been fixed in advance, we think that it should also be regarded as an open one for the consideration of the Congress when, in the presence of certified ratifications by three-fourths of the States, the time arrives for the promulgation of the adoption of the amendment. The decision by the Congress, in its control of the action of the Secretary of State, of the question whether the amendment had been adopted within a reasonable time would not be subject to review by the courts.

It would unduly lengthen this opinion to attempt to review our decisions as to the class of questions deemed to be political and not justiciable. In determining whether a question falls within that category, the appropriateness under our system of government of attributing finality to the action of the political departments and also the lack of satisfactory criteria for a judicial determination are dominant considerations.[30] There are many illustrations in the field of our conduct of foreign relations, where there are "considerations of policy, considerations of extreme magnitude, and certainly, entirely incompetent to the examination and decision of a court of justice." *Ware* v. *Hylton*, 3 Dall. 199, 260.[31] Questions involving similar considerations are found in the government of our internal affairs. Thus, under Article IV, § 4, of the Constitution, providing that the United States "shall guarantee to every State in this Union a Republican Form of Government," we have held that it rests with the Congress to decide what government is the established one in a State and whether or not it is republican in form. *Luther* v. *Borden*, 7 How. 1, 42. In that case Chief Justice Taney observed that "when the senators and representatives of a State are admitted into the councils of the Union, the authority of the government under which they are appointed, as well as its republican character, is recognized by the proper constitutional authority. And its decision is binding on every other department of the government, and could not be questioned in a judicial tribunal.'' So, it was held in the same case that under the provision of the same Article for the protection of each of the States ''against domestic violence'' it rested with the Congress ''to determine upon the means proper to be adopted to fulfil this guarantee.'' *Id.*, p. 43. So, in *Pacific Telephone Co.* v. *Oregon*, 223 U.S. 118, we considered that questions arising under the guaranty of a republican form of government had long since been ''definitely determined to be political and governmental'' and hence that the question whether the government of Oregon had ceased to be republican in form because of a constitutional amendment by which the people reserved to themselves power to propose and enact laws independently of the legislative assembly and also to approve or reject any act of that body, was a question for the determination of the Congress. It would be finally settled when the Congress admitted the senators and representatives of the State.

For the reasons we have stated, which we think to be as compelling as those which underlay the cited decisions, we think that the Congress in controlling the promulgation of the adoption of a constitutional amendment has the final determination of the question whether by lapse of time its proposal of the amendment had lost its vitality prior to the required ratifications. The state officials should not be restrained from certifying to the Secretary of State the adoption by the legislature of Kansas of the resolution of ratification.

As we find no reason for disturbing the decision of the Supreme Court of Kansas in denying the mandamus sought by petitioners, its judgment is affirmed but upon the grounds stated in this opinion.

Affirmed.

Notes

1. The text of the proposed amendment is as follows (43 Stat. 670):

''Section 1. The Congress shall have power to limit, regulate, and prohibit the labor of persons under eighteen years of age.

Sec. 2. The power of the several States is unimpaired by this article except that the operation of State laws shall be suspended to the extent necessary to give effect to legislation enacted by the Congress.''

2. The state court said on this point:

''At the threshold we are confronted with the question raised by the defendants as to the right of the plaintiffs to maintain this action. It appears that on March 30, 1937, the state senate adopted a resolution directing the attorney general to appear for the state of Kansas in this action. It further appears that on April 3, 1937, on application of the attorney general, an order was entered making the state of Kansas a party defendant. The state being a party to the proceedings, we think the right of the parties to maintain the action is beyond question. (G.S. 1935, 75–702; *State, ex rel.* v. *Public Service Comn.*, 135 Kan. 491, 11 P. 2d 999.)''

3. See *Caffrey* v. *Oklahoma Territory*, 177 U.S. 346; *Smith* v. *Indiana*, 191 U.S. 138; *Braxton County Court* v. *West Virginia*, 208 U.S. 192; *Marshall* v. *Dye*, 231 U.S. 250; *Stewart* v. *Kansas City*, 239 U.S. 14; *Columbus & Greenville Ry. Co.* v. *Miller*, 283 U.S. 96.

4. Mr. Justice Brandeis.

5. *Id.*, pp. 129, 130. See, also, *Frothingham* v. *Mellon*, 262 U.S. 447, 480, 486, 487.

6. *Pawhuska* v. *Pawhuska Oil Co.*, 250 U.S. 394; *Trenton* v. *New Jersey*, 262 U.S. 182; *Risty* v. *Chicago, R.I. & P. Ry. Co.*, 270 U.S. 378; *Williams* v. *Mayor*, 289 U.S. 36.

7. Act of October 22, 1913, 38 Stat. 219; 28 U.S. C. 47, 47a, 345.

8. 15 U.S. C. 45; 28 U.S.C. 348.

9. 29 U.S.C. 160 (e). See, also, as to orders of Federal Communications Commission, 47 U.S.C. 402 (e).

10. 1 Stat. 73, 85, 86.

11. 38 Stat. 790; see, also, Act of September 6, 1916, 39 Stat. 726.

12. See cases cited in Note 3.

13. Jameson on Constitutional Conventions, §§ 576–581; Willoughby on the Constitution, § 329a.

14. Jameson, *op. cit.*, §§ 582–584; Willoughby, *op. cit.*, § 329a; Ames, ''Proposed Amendments to the Constitution,'' House Doc. No. 353, Pt. 2, 54th Cong., 2d Sess., pp. 299, 300.

15. 13 Stat. 774, 775; Jameson, *op. cit.*, § 576; Ames, *op. cit.*, p.300.

16. 15 Stat. 710.

17. Act of March 2, 1867, 14 Stat., p. 428. See *White* v. *Hart*, 13 Wall. 646, 652.

18. 15 Stat. 710.

19. 15 Stat. 707.

20. Cong. Globe, 40th Cong., 2d Sess., p. 3857.

21. Cong. Globe, 40th Cong., 2d Sess., p. 4070.

22. 15 Stat. 706, 707.

23. 15 Stat. 709, 710.

24. 15 Stat. 710, 711; Ames, *op. cit.*, App. No. 1140, p. 377.

25. The legislature of New York which had ratified the Fifteenth Amendment in 1869 attempted, in January, 1870, to withdraw its ratifica-

tion, and while this fact was stated in the proclamation by Secretary Fish of the ratification of the amendment, and New York was not needed to make up the required three-fourths, that State was included in the list of ratifying States. 16 Stat. 1131; Ames, *op. cit.*, App. No. 1284, p. 388.

26. Compare Article VII.

27. 5 U.S.C. 160. From Act of April 20, 1818, § 2; 3 Stat. 439; R.S. § 205.

28. Sen. Rep. 726, 75th Cong., 1st Sess.; Sen. Rep. 788, 75th Cong., 1st Sess.: Letter of the President on January 8, 1937, to the Governors of nineteen non-ratifying States whose legislatures were to meet in that year, urging them to press for ratification. New York Times, January 9, 1937, p. 5.

29. 40 Stat. 1050. A similar provision was inserted in the Twenty-first Amendment. *United States* v. *Chambers*, 291 U.S. 217, 222.

30. See Willoughby, *op. cit.*, pp. 1326, *et seq.*; Oliver P. Field, "The Doctrine of Political Questions in the Federal Courts," 8 Minnesota Law Review, 485; Melville Fuller Weston, "Political Questions," 38 Harvard Law Review, 296.

31. See, also, *United States* v. *Palmer*, 3 Wheat. 610, 634; *Foster* v. *Neilson*, 2 Pet. 253, 309; *Doe* v. *Braden*, 16 How. 635, 657; *Terlinden* v. *Ames*, 184 U.S. 270, 288.

b. CONCURRING OPINION BY MR. JUSTICE BLACK,
IN WHICH MR. JUSTICE ROBERTS, MR. JUSTICE FRANKFURTER
AND MR. JUSTICE DOUGLAS JOIN.

Although, for reasons to be stated by MR. JUSTICE FRANKFURTER, we believe this cause should be dismissed, the ruling of the Court just announced removes from the case the question of petitioners' standing to sue. Under the compulsion of that ruling,[1] MR. JUSTICE ROBERTS, MR. JUSTICE FRANKFURTER, MR. JUSTICE DOUGLAS and I have participated in the discussion of other questions considered by the Court and we concur in the result reached, but for somewhat different reasons.

The Constitution grants Congress exclusive power to control submission of constitutional amendments. Final determination by Congress that ratification by three-fourths of the States has taken place "is conclusive upon the courts."[2] In the exercise of that power, Congress, of course, is governed by the Constitution. However, whether submission, intervening procedure or Congressional determination of ratification conforms to the commands of the Constitution, calls for decisions by a "political department" of questions of a type which this Court has frequently designated "political." And decision of a "political question" by the "political department" to which the Constitution has committed it "conclusively binds the judges, as well as all other officers, citizens and subjects of . . . government."[3] Proclamation under authority of Congress that an amendment has been ratified will carry with it a solemn assurance by the Congress that ratification has taken place as the Constitution commands. Upon this assurance a proclaimed amendment must be accepted as a part of the Constitution, leaving to the judiciary its traditional authority of interpretation.[4] To the extent that the Court's opinion in the present case even impliedly assumes a power to make judicial interpretation of the exclusive constitutional authority of Congress over submission and ratification of amendments, we are unable to agree.

The state court below assumed jurisdiction to determine whether the proper procedure is being followed between submission and final adoption. However, it is apparent that judicial review of or pronouncements upon a supposed limitation of a "reasonable time" within which Congress may accept ratification; as to whether duly authorized state officials have proceeded properly in ratifying or voting for ratification; or whether a State may reverse its action once taken upon a proposed amendment; and kindred questions, are all consistent only with an ultimate control over the amending process in the courts. And this must inevitably embarrass the course of amendment by subjecting to judicial interference matters that we believe were intrusted by the Constitution solely to the political branch of government.

The Court here treats the amending process of the Constitution in some respects as subject to judicial construction, in others as subject to the final authority of the Congress. There is no disapproval of the conclusion arrived at in *Dillon* v. *Gloss*,[5] that the Constitution impliedly requires that a properly submitted amendment must die unless ratified within a "reasonable time." Nor does the Court now disapprove its prior assumption of power to make such a pronouncement. And it is not made clear that only Congress has constitutional power to determine if there is any such implication in Article V of the Constitution. On the other hand, the Court's opinion declares that Congress has the exclusive power to decide the "political questions" of whether a State whose legislature has once acted upon a proposed amendment may subsequently reverse its position, and whether, in the circumstances of such a case as this, an amendment is dead because an "unreasonable" time has elapsed. No such division between the political and judicial branches of the government is made by Article V which grants power over the amending of the Constitution to Congress alone. Undivided control of that process has been given by the Article exclusively and completely to Congress. The process itself is "political" in its entirety, from submission until an amendment becomes part of the Constitution, and is not subject to judicial guidance, control or interference at any point.

Since Congress has sole and complete control over the amending process, subject to no judicial review, the views of any court upon this process cannot be binding upon Congress, and insofar as *Dillon* v. *Gloss* attempts judicially to impose a limitation upon the right of Congress to determine final adoption of an amendment, it should be disapproved. If Congressional determination that an amendment has been completed and become a part of the Constitution is final and removed from examination by the courts, as the Court's present opinion recognizes, surely the steps leading to that condition must be subject to the scrutiny, control and appraisal of none save the Congress, the body having exclusive power to make that final determination.

Congress, possessing exclusive power over the amending process, cannot be bound by and is under no duty to accept the pronouncements upon that exclusive power by this Court or by the Kansas courts. Neither state nor federal courts can review that power. Therefore, any judicial expression amounting to more than mere acknowledgment of exclusive Congressional power over the political process of amendment is a mere admonition to the Congress in the nature of an advisory opinion, given wholly without constitutional authority.

Notes

1. Cf., *Helvering* v. *Davis*, 301 U.S. 619, 639–40.

2. *Leser* v. *Garnett*, 258 U.S. 130, 137.

3. *Jones* v. *United States*, 137 U.S. 202, 212; *Foster* v. *Neilson*, 2 Pet. 253, 309, 314; *Luther* v. *Borden*, 7 How. 1, 42; *In re Cooper*, 143 U.S. 472, 503; *Pacific States Telephone Co.* v. *Oregon*, 223 U.S. 118; *Davis* v. *Ohio*, 241 U.S. 565, 569. "And in this view, it is not material to inquire, nor is it the province of the court to determine, whether the executive ["political department"] be right or wrong. It is enough to know that in the exercise of his constitutional functions, he had decided the question. Having done this, under the responsibilities which belong to him, it is obligatory on the people and government of the Union. . . . this court have laid down the rule, that the action of the political branches of the government in a matter that belongs to them, is conclusive." *Williams* v. *Suffolk Ins. Co.*, 13 Pet. 415, 420.

4. *Field* v. *Clark*, 143 U.S. 649, 672.

5. 256 U.S. 368, 375.

c. OPINION BY MR. JUSTICE FRANKFURTER.

It is the view of MR. JUSTICE ROBERTS, MR. JUSTICE BLACK, MR. JUSTICE DOUGLAS and myself that the petitioners have no standing in this Court.

In endowing this Court with "judicial Power" the Constitution presupposed an historic content for that phrase and relied on assumption by the judiciary of authority only over issues which are appropriate for disposition by judges. The Constitution further explicitly indicated the limited area within which judicial action was to move—however far-reaching the consequences of action within that area—by extending "judicial Power" only to "Cases" and "Controversies." Both by what they said and by what they implied, the framers of the Judiciary Article gave merely the outlines of what were to them the familiar operations of the English judicial system and its manifestations on this side of the ocean before the Union. Judicial power could come into play only in matters that were the traditional concern of the courts at Westminster and only if they arose in ways that to the expert feel of lawyers constituted "Cases" or "Controversies." It was not for courts to meddle with matters that required no subtlety to be identified as political issues.[1] And even as to the kinds of questions which were the staple of judicial business, it was not for courts to pass upon them as abstract, intellectual problems but only if a concrete, living contest between adversaries called for the arbitrament of law. Compare *Muskrat* v. *United States*, 219 U.S. 346; *Tutun* v. *United States*, 270 U.S. 568; *Willing* v. *Chicago Auditorium Assn.*, 277 U.S. 274; *Nashville, C. & St. L. Ry. Co.* v. *Wallace*, 288 U.S. 249.

As abstractions, these generalities represent common ground among judges. Since, however, considerations governing the exercise of judicial power are not mechanical criteria but derive from conceptions regarding the distribution of governmental powers in their manifold, changing guises, differences in the application of canons of jurisdiction have arisen from the beginning of the Court's history.[2] Conscious or unconscious leanings toward the serviceability of the judicial process in the adjustment of public controversies clothed in the form of private litigation inevitably affect decisions. For they influence awareness in recognizing the relevance of conceded doctrines of judicial self-limitation and rigor in enforcing them.

Of all this, the present controversy furnishes abundant illustration. Twenty-one members of the Kansas Senate and three members of its House of Representatives brought an original mandamus proceeding in the Supreme Court of that State to compel the Secretary of its Senate to erase an endorsement on Kansas "Senate Concurrent Resolution No. 3" of January 1937, to the effect that it had been passed by the Senate, and instead to endorse thereon the words "not passed." They also sought to restrain the officers of both Senate and House from authenticating and delivering it to the Governor of the State for transmission to the Secretary of State of the United States. These Kansas legislators resorted to their Supreme Court claiming that there was no longer an amendment open for ratification by Kansas and that, in any event, it had not been ratified by the "legislature" of Kansas, the constitutional organ for such ratification. See Article V of the Constitution of the United States. The Kansas Supreme Court held that the Kansas legislators had a right to its judgment on these claims, but on the merits decided against them and denied a writ of mandamus. Urging that such denial was in derogation of their rights under the Federal Constitution, the legislators, having been granted *certiorari* to review the Kansas judgment, 303 U.S. 632, ask this Court to reverse it.

Our power to do so is explicitly challenged by the United States as *amicus curiae*, but would in any event have to be faced. See *Mansfield, C. & L.M. Ry. Co.* v. *Swan*, 111 U.S. 379, 382. To whom and for what causes the courts of Kansas are open are matters for Kansas to determine.[3] But Kansas can not define the contours of the authority of the federal courts, and more particularly of this Court. It is our ultimate responsibility to determine who may invoke our judgment and under what circumstances. Are these members of the Kansas legislature, therefore, entitled to ask us to adjudicate the grievances of which they complain?

It is not our function, and it is beyond our power, to write legal essays or to give legal opinions, however solemnly requested and however great the national emergency. See the correspondence between Secretary of State Jefferson and Chief Justice Jay, 3 Johnson, Correspondence and Public Papers of John Jay, 486–89. Unlike the rôle allowed to judges in a few state courts and to the Supreme Court of Canada, our exclusive business is litigation.[4] The requisites of litigation are not satisfied when questions of constitutionality though conveyed through the outward forms of a conventional court proceeding do not bear special relation to a particular litigant. The scope and consequences of our doctrine of judicial review over executive and legislative action should make us observe fastidiously the bounds of the litigious process within which we are confined.[5] No matter how seriously infringement of the Constitution may be called into question, this is not the tribunal for its challenge except by those who have some specialized interest of their own to vindicate, apart from a political concern which belongs to all. *Stearns* v. *Wood*, 236 U.S. 75; *Fairchild* v. *Hughes*, 258 U.S. 126.

In the familiar language of jurisdiction, these Kansas legislators must have standing in this Court. What is their distinctive claim to be here, not possessed by every Kansan? What is it that they complain of, which could not be complained of here by all their fellow citizens? The answer requires analysis of the grievances which they urge.

They say that it was beyond the power of the Kansas legislature, no matter who voted or how, to ratify the Child Labor Amendment because for Kansas there was no Child Labor Amendment to ratify. Assuming that an amendment proposed by the Congress dies of inanition after what is to be deemed a "reasonable" time, they claim that, having been submitted in 1924, the proposed Child Labor Amendment was no longer alive in 1937. Or, if alive, it was no longer so for Kansas because, by a prior resolution of rejection in 1925, Kansas had exhausted her power. In no respect, however, do these objections relate to any secular interest that pertains to these Kansas legislators apart from interests that belong to the entire commonalty of Kansas. The fact that these legislators are part of the ratifying mechanism while the ordinary citizen of Kansas is not, is wholly irrelevant to this issue. On this aspect of the case the problem would be exactly the same if all but one legislator had voted for ratification.

Indeed the claim that the Amendment was dead or that it was no longer open to Kansas to ratify, is not only not an interest which belongs uniquely to these Kansas legislators; it is not even an interest special to Kansas. For it is the common concern of every citizen of the United States whether the Amendment is still alive, or whether Kansas could be included among the necessary "three-fourths of the several States."

These legislators have no more standing on these claims of unconstitutionality to attack "Senate Concurrent Resolution No. 3" than they would have standing here to attack some Kansas statute claimed by them to offend the Commerce Clause. By as much right could a member of the Congress who had voted against the passage of a bill because moved by constitutional scruples urge before this Court our duty to consider his arguments of unconstitutionality.

Clearly a Kansan legislator would have no standing had he brought suit in a federal court. Can the Kansas Supreme Court transmute the general interest in these constitutional claims into the individualized legal interest indispensable here? No doubt the bounds of such legal interest have a penumbra which gives some freedom in judging fulfilment of our jurisdictional requirements. The doctrines affecting standing to sue in the federal courts will not be treated as mechanical yardsticks in assessing state court ascertainments of legal interest brought here for review. For the creation of a vast domain of legal interests is in the keeping of the states, and from time to time state courts and legislators give legal protection to new individual interests. Thus, while the ordinary state taxpayer's suit is not recognized in the federal courts, it affords adequate standing for review of state decisions when so recognized by state courts. *Coyle* v. *Smith*, 221 U.S. 559; *Heim* v. *McCall*, 239 U.S. 175.

But it by no means follows that a state court ruling on the adequacy of legal interest is binding here. Thus, in *Tyler* v. *Judges*, 179 U.S. 405, the notion was rejected that merely because the Supreme Judicial Court of Massachusetts found an interest of sufficient legal significance for assailing a statute, this Court must consider such claim. Again, this Court has consistently held that the interest of a state official in vindicating the Constitution of the United States gives him no legal standing here to attack the constitutionality of a state statute in order to avoid compliance with it. *Smith* v. *Indiana*, 191 U.S. 138; *Braxton County Court* v. *West Virginia*, 208 U.S. 192; *Marshall* v. *Dye*, 231 U.S. 250; *Stewart* v. *Kansas City*, 239 U.S. 14. Nor can recognition by a state court of such an undifferentiated, general interest confer jurisdiction on us. *Columbus & Greenville Ry. Co.* v. *Miller*, 283 U.S. 96, reversing *Miller* v. *Columbus & Greenville Ry.*, 154 Miss. 317; 122 So. 366. Contrariwise, of course, an official has a legally recognized duty to enforce a statute which he is charged with enforcing. And so, an official who is obstructed in the performance of his duty under a state statute because his state court found a violation of the United States Constitution may, since the Act of December 23, 1914, 38 Stat. 790, ask this Court to remove the fetters against enforcement of his duty imposed by the state court because of an asserted misconception of the Constitution. Such a situation is represented by *Blodgett* v. *Silberman*, 277 U.S. 1, and satisfied the requirement of legal interest in *Boynton* v. *Hutcheson*, 291 U.S. 656, *certiorari* dismissed on another ground in 292 U.S. 601.[6]

We can only adjudicate an issue as to which there is a claimant before us who has a special, individualized stake in it. One who is merely the self-constituted spokesman of a constitutional point of view can not ask us to pass on it. The Kansas legislators could not bring suit explicitly on behalf of the people of the United States to determine whether Kansas could still vote for the Child Labor Amendment. They can not gain standing here by having brought such a suit in their own names. Therefore, none of the petitioners can here raise questions concerning the power of the Kansas legislature to ratify the Amendment.

This disposes of the standing of the three members of the lower house who seek to invoke the jurisdiction of this Court. They have no standing here. Equally without litigious standing is the member of the Kansas Senate who voted for "Senate Concurrent Resolution No. 3." He cannot claim that his vote was denied any parliamentary efficacy to which it was entitled. There remains for consideration only the claim of the twenty nay-voting senators that the Lieutenant-Governor of Kansas, the presiding officer of its Senate, had, under the Kansas Constitution, no power to break the tie in the senatorial vote on the Amendment, thereby depriving their votes of the effect of creating such a tie. Whether this is the tribunal before which such a question can be raised by these senators must be determined even before considering whether the issue which they pose is justiciable. For the latter involves questions affecting the distribution of constitutional power which should be postponed to preliminary questions of legal standing to sue.

The right of the Kansas senators to be here is rested on recognition by *Leser* v. *Garnett*, 258 U.S. 130, of a voter's right to protect his franchise. The historic source of this doctrine and the reasons for it were explained in *Nixon* v. *Herndon*, 273 U.S. 536, 540. That was an action for $5,000 damages against the Judges of Elections for refusing to permit the plaintiff to vote at a primary election in Texas. In disposing of the objection that the plaintiff had no cause of action because the subject matter of the suit was political, Mr. Justice Holmes thus spoke for the Court: "Of course the petition concerns political action but it alleges and seeks to recover for private damage. That private damage may be caused by such political action and may be recovered for in a suit at law hardly has been doubted for over two hundred years, since *Ashby* v. *White*, 2 Ld. Raym. 938, 3 *id*. 320, and has been recognized by this Court." "Private damage" is the clue to the famous ruling in *Ashby* v. *White, supra*, and determines its scope as well as that of cases in this Court of which it is the justification. The judgment of Lord Holt is permeated with the conception that a voter's franchise is a personal right, assessable in money damages, of which the exact amount "is peculiarly appropriate for the determination of a jury," see *Wiley* v. *Sinkler*, 179 U.S. 58, 65, and for which there is no remedy outside the law courts. "Although this matter relates to the parliament," said Lord Holt, "yet it is an injury precedaneous to the parliament, as my Lord Hale said in the case of *Bernardiston* v. *Soame*, 2 Lev. 114, 116. The parliament cannot judge of this injury, nor give damage to the plaintiff for it: they cannot make him a recompense." 2 Ld. Raym. 938, 958.

The reasoning of *Ashby* v. *White* and the practice which has followed it leave intra-parliamentary controversies to parliaments and outside the scrutiny of law courts. The procedures for voting in legislative assemblies— who are members, how and when they should vote, what is the requisite number of votes for different phases of legislative activity, what votes were cast and how they were counted—surely are matters that not merely concern political action but are of the very essence of political action, if "political" has any connotation at all. *Field* v. *Clark*, 143 U.S. 649, 670, *et seq.; Leser* v. *Garnett*, 258 U.S. 130, 137. In no sense are they matters of "private damage." They pertain to legislators not as individuals but as political representatives executing the legislative process. To open the law courts to such controversies is to have courts sit in judgment on the manifold disputes engendered by procedures for voting in legislative assemblies. If the doctrine of *Ashby* v. *White* vindicating the private rights of a voting citizen has not been doubted for over two hundred years, it is equally significant that for over two hundred years *Ashby* v. *White* has not been sought to be put to purposes like the present. In seeking redress here these Kansas senators have wholly misconceived the functions of this Court. The writ of *certiorari* to the Kansas Supreme Court should therefore be dismissed.

Notes

1. For an early instance of the abstention of the King's Justices from matters political, see the Duke of York's Claim to the Crown, House of Lords, 1460, 5 Rot. Parl. 375, reprinted in Wambaugh, Cases on Constitutional Law, 1.

2. See *e.g.* the opinion of Mr. Justice Iredell in *Chisholm* v. *Georgia*, 2 Dall. 419, 429; concurring opinion of Mr. Justice Johnson in *Fletcher* v. *Peck*, 6 Cranch 87, 143; and the cases collected in the concurring opinion of Mr. Justice Brandeis in *Ashwander* v. *Tennessee Valley Authority*, 297 U.S. 288, 341.

3. This is subject to some narrow exceptions not here relevant. See, e.g., *McKnett* v. *St. Louis & S. F. Ry. Co.*, 292 U.S. 230.

4. As to advisory opinions in use in a few of the state courts, see J. B. Thayer, Advisory Opinions, reprinted in Legal Essays by J. B. Thayer, at 42 *et seq.*; article on "Advisory Opinions," 1 Enc. Soc. Sci. 475. As to advisory opinions in Canada, see *Attorney-General for Ontario* v. *Attorney-General for Canada* [1912] A.C. 571. Speaking of the Canadian system, Lord Chancellor Haldane, in *Attorney-General for British Columbia* v. *Attorney General for Canada* [1914] A.C. 153, 162, said: "It is at times attended with inconveniences, and it is not surprising that the Supreme Court of the United States should have steadily refused to adopt a similar procedure, and should have confined itself to adjudication on the legal rights of litigants in actual controversies." For further animadversions on advisory pronounce-

ments by judges, see Lord Chancellor Sankey in *In re The Regulation and Control of Aeronautics in Canada* [1932] A.C. 54, 66: "We sympathize with the view expressed at length by Newcombe, J., which was concurred in by the Chief Justice, [of Canada] as to the difficulty which the Court must experience in endeavoring to answer questions put to it in this way."

Australia followed our Constitutional practice in restricting her courts to litigious business. The experience of English history which lay behind it was thus put in the Australian Constitutional Convention by Mr. (later Mr. Justice) Higgins: "I feel strongly that it is most inexpedient to break in on the established practice of the English law, and secure decisions on facts which have not arisen yet. Of course, it is a matter that lawyers have experience of every day, that a judge does not give the same attention, he can not give that same attention, to a suppositious case as when he feels the pressure of the consequences to a litigant before him. . . . But here is an attempt to allow this High Court, before cases have arisen, to make a pronouncement upon the law that will be binding. I think the imagination of judges, like that of other persons, is limited, and they are not able to put before their minds all the complex circumstances which may arise and which they ought to have in their minds when giving a decision. If there is one thing more than another which is recognized in British jurisprudence it is that a judge never gives a decision until the facts necessary for that decision have arisen." Rep. Nat. Austral. Conv. Deb. (1897) 966–67.

5. See the series of cases beginning with *Hayburn's Case*, 2 Dall. 409, through *United States* v. *West Virginia*, 295 U.S. 463.

6. A quick summary of the jurisdiction of this Court over state court decisions leaves no room for doubt that the fact that the present case is here on *certiorari* is wholly irrelevant to our assumption of jurisdiction. Section 25 of the First Judiciary Act gave reviewing power to this Court only over state court decisions *denying* a claim of federal right. This restriction was, of course, born of fear of disobedience by the state judiciaries of national authority. The Act of September 6, 1916, 39 Stat. 726, withdrew from this obligatory jurisdiction cases where the state decision was against a "title, right, privilege, or immunity" claimed to exist under the Constitution, laws, treaties or authorities of the United States. This change, which was inspired mainly by a desire to eliminate from review as of right cases arising under the Federal Employers' Liability Act, left such review only in cases where the validity of a treaty, statute or authority of the United States was drawn into question and the decision was against the validity, and in cases where the validity of a statute of a state or a state authority was drawn into question on the grounds of conflict with federal law and the decision was in favor of

its validity. The Act of February 13, 1925, 43 Stat. 936, 937, extended this process of restricting our obligatory jurisdiction by transferring to review by *certiorari* cases in which the state court had held invalid an "authority" claimed to be exercised under the laws of the United States or in which it had upheld, against claims of invalidity on federal grounds, an "authority" exercised under the laws of the states. Neither the terms of these two restrictions nor the controlling comments in committee reports or by members of this Court who had a special share in promoting the Acts of 1916 and 1925, give any support for believing that by contracting the range of obligatory jurisdiction over state adjudications Congress enlarged the jurisdiction of the Court by removing the established requirement of legal interest as a threshold condition to being here.

Nor does the Act of December 23, 1914, 38 Stat. 790, touch the present problem. By that Act, Congress for the first time gave this Court power to review state court decisions *sustaining* a federal right. For this purpose it made *certiorari* available. The Committee reports and the debates on this Act prove that its purpose was merely to remove the unilateral quality of Supreme Court review of state court decisions on constitutional questions as to which this Court has the ultimate say. The Act did not create a new legal interest as a basis of review here; it built on the settled doctrine that an official has a legally recognizable duty to carry out a statute which he is supposed to enforce.

Thus, prior to the Act of 1914, the Kentucky case, *post*, p. 474, could not have come here at all, and prior to 1916, the Kansas case would have come here, if at all, by writ of error. By allowing cases from state courts which previously could not have come here at all to come here on *certiorari* the Act of 1914 merely lifted the previous bar—that a federal claim had been sustained—but left every other requisite of jurisdiction unchanged. Similarly, no change in these requisites was affected by the Acts of 1916 and 1925 in confining certain categories of litigation from the state courts to our discretionary instead of obligatory reviewing power.

d. MR. JUSTICE BUTLER, DISSENTING.

The Child Labor Amendment was proposed in 1924; more than 13 years elapsed before the Kansas legislature voted, as the decision just announced holds, to ratify it. Petitioners insist that more than a reasonable time had elapsed and that, therefore, the action of the state legislature is without force. But this Court now holds that the question is not justiciable, relegates it to the "consideration of the Congress when, in the presence of certified ratifications by three-fourths of the States the time arrives for the promulgation of the adoption of the amendment'' and declares that the decision by Congress would not be subject to review by the courts.

In *Dillon* v. *Gloss*, 256 U.S. 368, one imprisoned for transportation of intoxicating liquor in violation of § 3 of the National Prohibition Act, instituted habeas corpus preceedings to obtain his release on the ground that the Eighteenth Amendment was invalid because the resolution proposing it declared that it should not be operative unless ratified within seven years. The Amendment was ratified in less than a year and a half. We definitely held that Article V impliedly requires amendments submitted to be ratified within a reasonable time after proposal; that Congress may fix a reasonable time for ratification, and that the period of seven years fixed by the Congress was reasonable.

We said:

"It will be seen that this article says nothing about the time within which ratification may be had—neither that it shall be unlimited nor that it shall be fixed by Congress. What, then, is the reasonable inference or implication? Is it that ratification may be had at any time, as within a few years, a century or even a longer period; or that it must be had within some reasonable period which Congress is left free to define?

We do not find anything in the Article which suggests that an amendment once proposed is to be open to ratification for all time, or that ratification in some of the States may be separated from that in others by many years and yet be effective. We do find that which strongly suggests the contrary. First, proposal and ratification are not treated as unrelated acts, but as succeeding steps in a single endeavor, the natural inference being that they are not to be widely separated in time. Secondly, it is only when there is deemed to be a necessity therefor that amendments are to be proposed, the reasonable implication being that when proposed they are to be considered and disposed of presently. Thirdly, as ratification is but the expression of the approbation of the people and is to be effective when had in three-fourths of the States, there is a fair implication that it must be sufficiently contemporaneous in that number of States to reflect the will of the people in all sections at relatively the same period, which of course ratification scattered through a long series of years would not do. These considerations and the general purport and spirit of the Article lead to the conclusion expressed by Judge Jameson [in his Constitutional Conventions, 4th ed. § 585] "that an alteration of the Constitution proposed today has relation to the sentiment and the felt needs of today, and that, if not ratified early while that sentiment may fairly be supposed to exist, it ought to be regarded as waived, and not again to be voted upon, unless a second time proposed by Congress.'' That this is the better conclusion becomes even more manifest when what is comprehended in the other view is considered; for, according to it, four amendments proposed long ago—two in 1789, one in 1810, and one in 1861—are still pending and in a situation where their ratification in some of the States many years since by representatives of generations now largely forgotten may be effectively supplemented in enough more States to make three-fourths by representatives of the present or some future generation. To that view few would be able to subscribe, and in our opinion it is quite untenable. We conclude that the fair inference or implication from Article V is that the ratification must be within some reasonable time after the proposal.

Of the power of Congress, keeping within reasonable limits, to fix a definite period for the ratification we entertain no doubt.... Whether a definite period for ratification shall be fixed so that all may know what it is and speculation on what is a reasonable time may be avoided, is, in our opinion, a matter of detail which Congress may determine as an incident of its power to designate the mode of ratification. It is not questioned that seven years, the period fixed in this instance, was reasonable, if power existed to fix a definite time; nor could it well be questioned considering the periods within which prior amendments were ratified.''

Upon the reasoning of our opinion in that case, I would hold that more than a reasonable time had elapsed* and that the judgment of the Kansas supreme court should be reversed.

The point that the question—whether more than a reasonable time had elapsed—is not justiciable but one for Congress after attempted ratification by the requisite number of States, was not raised by the parties or by the United States appearing as *amicus curiae*; it was not suggested by us when ordering reargument. As the Court, in the *Dillon* case, did directly decide upon the reasonableness of the seven years fixed by the Congress, it ought not now, without hearing argument upon the point, hold itself to lack power to decide whether more than 13 years between proposal by Congress and attempted ratification by Kansas is reasonable.

MR. JUSTICE McREYNOLDS joins in this opinion.

* CHRONOLOGY OF CHILD LABOR AMENDMENT.

[A State is said to have ''rejected'' when both Houses of its legislature passed resolutions of rejection, and to have ''refused to ratify'' when both Houses defeated resolution for ratification.] *(note cont. p. 138)*

7. Excerpts from *Baker* v. *Carr*, 369 U.S. 186 (1962)

[Appeal from a denial to overturn Tennessee's Apportionment Act of 1901 and force reapportionment of the General Assembly. The district court held that it lacked jurisdiction of the subject matter and that plaintiffs had failed to state a claim upon which relief could be granted. Mr. Justice Brennan delivered the opinion of the court.]

In the setting of a case such as this, the recited grounds embrace two possible reasons for dismissal:

First: That the facts and injury alleged, the legal bases invoked as creating the rights and duties relied upon, and the relief sought, fail to come within that language of Article III of the Constitution and of the jurisdictional statutes which define those matters concerning which United States District Courts are empowered to act;

Second: That, although the matter is cognizable and facts are alleged

---

(note, cont.)

June 2, 1924, Joint Resolution deposited in State Department. In that year, Arkansas ratified; North Carolina rejected. *Ratification, 1; rejection, 1.*

1925, Arizona, California and Wisconsin ratified; Florida, Georgia, Indiana, Kansas, Maine, Massachusetts, Minnesota, Missouri, New Hampshire, Pennsylvania, South Carolina, Tennessee, Texas, Utah, and Vermont rejected; Connecticut, Delaware and South Dakota refused to ratify. *Ratifications, 4; rejections, 16; refusals to ratify, 3.*

1926, Kentucky and Virginia rejected. *Ratifications, 4; rejections, 18; refusals to ratify, 3.*

1927, Montana, ratified; Maryland rejected. *Ratifications, 5; rejections, 19; refusals to ratify, 3.*

1931, Colorado ratified. *Ratifications, 6; rejections, 19; refusals to ratify, 3.*

1933, Illinois, Iowa, Michigan, New Jersey, North Dakota, Ohio, Oklahoma, Oregon, Washington and West Virginia ratified as did also Maine, Minnesota, New Hampshire, and Pennsylvania, which had rejected in 1925. *Ratifications, 20; rejections, (eliminating States subsequently ratifying) 15; refusals to ratify, 3.*

1935, Idaho and Wyoming ratified, as did Utah and Indiana, which had rejected in 1925. As in 1925, Connecticut refused to ratify. *Ratifications, 24; rejections, 13; refusals to ratify, 3.*

1936, Kentucky, which had rejected in 1926, ratified. *Ratifications, 25; rejections, 12; refusals to ratify, 3.*

1937, Nevada and New Mexico ratified, as did Kansas, which had rejected in 1925. Massachusetts, which had rejected in 1925, refused to ratify. *Ratifications, 28; rejections, 11; refusals to ratify, 3.*

Six States are not included in this list: Alabama, Louisiana, Mississippi, Nebraska, New York and Rhode Island. It appears that there has never been a vote in Alabama or Rhode Island. Louisiana house of representatives has three times (1924, 1934 and 1936) defeated resolutions for ratification. In Mississippi, the Senate adopted resolution for ratification in 1934, but in 1936 another Senate resolution for ratification was adversely reported. In Nebraska, the House defeated ratification resolutions in 1927 and 1935, but the Senate passed such a resolution in 1929. In New York, ratification was defeated in the House in 1935 and 1937, and in the latter year, the Senate passed such a resolution.

which establish infringement of appellants' rights as a result of state legislative action departing from a federal constitutional standard, the court will not proceed because the matter is considered unsuited to judicial inquiry or adjustment.

We treat the first ground of dismissal as "lack of jurisdiction of the subject matter." The second we consider to result in a failure to state a justiciable cause of action.

The District Court's dismissal order recited that it was issued in conformity with the court's *per curiam* opinion. The opinion reveals that the court rested its dismissal upon lack of subject-matter jurisdiction and lack of a justiciable cause of action without attempting to distinguish between these grounds. . . .

In light of the District Court's treatment of the case, we hold today only (a) that the court possessed jurisdiction of the subject matter; (b) that a justiciable cause of action is stated upon which appellants would be entitled to appropriate relief; and (c) because appellees raise the issue before this Court, that the appellants have standing to challenge the Tennessee apportionment statutes. Beyond noting that we have no cause at this stage to doubt the District Court will be able to fashion relief if violations of constitutional rights are found, it is improper now to consider what remedy would be most appropriate if appellants prevail at the trial.

II
Jurisdiction of the Subject Matter.

The District Court was uncertain whether our cases withholding federal judicial relief rested upon a lack of federal jurisdiction or upon the inappropriateness of the subject matter for judicial consideration—what we have designated "nonjusticiability." The distinction between the two grounds is significant. In the instance of nonjusticiability, consideration of the cause is not wholly and immediately foreclosed; rather, the Court's inquiry necessarily proceeds to the point of deciding whether the duty asserted can be judicially identified and its breach judicially determined, and whether protection for the right asserted can be judicially molded. In the instance of lack of jurisdiction the cause either does not "arise under" the Federal Constitution, laws or treaties (or fall within one of the other enumerated categories of Art. III, § 2), or is not a "case or controversy" within the meaning of that section; or the cause is not one described by any jurisdictional statute. Our conclusion, see pp. 208–237, *infra*, that this cause presents no nonjusticiable "political question" settles the only possible doubt that it is a case or controversy. Under the present heading of "Jurisdiction of the Subject Matter" we hold only that the matter set forth in the complaint does arise under the Constitution and is within 28 U.S.C. § 1343.

Article III, § 2, of the Federal Constitution provides that "The judicial Power shall extend to all Cases, in Law and Equity, arising under this Constitution, the Laws of the United States, and Treaties made, or which shall be made, under their Authority. . . ." It is clear that the cause of action is one which "arises under" the Federal Constitution. The complaint alleges that the 1901 statute effects an apportionment that deprives the appellants of the equal protection of the laws in violation of the Fourteenth Amendment. Dismissal of the complaint upon the ground of lack of jurisdiction of the subject matter would, therefore, be justified only if that claim were "so attenuated and unsubstantial as to be absolutely devoid of merit." . . . Since the District Court obviously and correctly did not deem the asserted federal constitutional claim unsubstantial and frivolous, it should not have dismissed the complaint for want of jurisdiction of the subject matter. . . .

An unbroken line of our precedents sustains the federal courts' jurisdiction of the subject matter of federal constitutional claims of this nature. . . .

III
Standing.

A federal court cannot "pronounce any statute, either of a State or of the United States, void, because irreconcilable with the Constitution, except as it is called upon to adjudge the legal rights of litigants in actual controversies." . . . Have the appellants alleged such a personal stake in the outcome of the controversy as to assure that concrete adverseness which sharpens the presentation of issues upon which the court so largely depends for illumination of difficult constitutional questions? This is the gist of the question of standing. It is, of course, a question of federal law. . . .

We hold that the appellants do have standing to maintain this suit. Our decisions plainly support this conclusion. Many of the cases have assumed rather than articulated the premise in deciding the merits of similar claims [footnote deleted]. . . .

. . . A citizen's right to a vote free of arbitrary impairment by state action has been judicially recognized as a right secured by the Constitution. . . .

. . . They are asserting "a plain, direct and adequate interest in maintaining the effectiveness of their votes," *Coleman* v. *Miller*, 307 U.S., at 438, not merely a claim of "the right, possessed by every citizen, to require that the Government be administered according to law. . . ." *Fairchild* v. *Hughes*, 258 U.S. 126, 129; compare *Leser* v. *Garnett*, 258 U.S. 130. They are entitled to a hearing and to the District Court's decision on their claims. . . .

IV
Justiciability.

In holding that the subject matter of this suit was not justiciable, the District Court relied on *Colegrove* v. *Green, supra,* and subsequent *per curiam cases* [footnote deleted]. . . . We understand the District Court to have read the cited cases as compelling the conclusion that since the appellants sought to have a legislative apportionment held unconstitutional, their suit presented a "political question" and was therefore nonjusticiable. We hold that this challenge to an apportionment presents no nonjusticiable "political question." The cited cases do not hold the contrary.

Of course the mere fact that the suit seeks protection of a political right does not mean it presents a political question. . . . Rather, it is argued that apportionment cases, whatever the actual wording of the complaint, can involve no federal constitutional right except one resting on the guaranty of a republican form of government [footnote deleted], and that complaints based on that clause have been held to present political questions which are nonjusticiable.

We hold that the claim pleaded here neither rests upon nor implicates the Guaranty Clause and that its justiciability is therefore not foreclosed by our decisions of cases involving that clause. . . . Appellants' claim that they are being denied equal protection is justiciable, and if "discrimination is sufficiently shown, the right to relief under the equal protection clause is not diminished by the fact that the discrimination relates to political rights." *Snowden* v. *Hughes*, 321 U.S. 1, 11. To show why we reject the argument based on the Guaranty Clause, we must examine the authorities under it. But because there appears to be some uncertainty as to why those cases did present political questions, and specifically as to whether this apportionment case is like those cases, we deem it necessary first to consider the contours of the "political question" doctrine.

Our discussion, even at the price of extending this opinion, requires review of a number of political question cases. . . . That review reveals that in the Guaranty Clause cases and in the other "political question" cases, it is the relationship between the judiciary and the coordinate branches of the Federal Government, and not the federal judiciary's relationship to the States, which gives rise to the "political question."

We have said that "In determining whether a question falls within [the political question] category, the approriateness under our system of government of attributing finality to the action of the political departments and also the lack of satisfactory criteria for a judicial determination are dominant considerations." *Coleman* v. *Miller*, 307 U.S. 433, 454–455. The nonjusticiability of a political question is primarily a function of the separation of powers. Much confusion results from the capacity of the "political question" label to obscure the need for case-by-case inquiry. Deciding whether a matter has in any measure been committed by the Constitution to another branch of government, or whether the action of that branch exceeds whatever authority has been committed, is itself a delicate exercise in constitutional interpretation, and is a responsibility of this Court as ultimate interpreter of the Constitution. To demonstrate this requires no less than to analyze representative cases and to infer from them the analytical threads that make up the political question doctrine. We shall then show that none of those threads catches this case.

Foreign relations: There are sweeping statements to the effect that all questions touching foreign relations are political questions. Not only does resolution of such issues frequently turn on standards that defy judicial application, or involve the exercise of a discretion demonstrably committed to the executive or legislature; but many such questions uniquely demand single-voiced statement of the Government's views. Yet it is error to suppose that every case or controversy which touches foreign relations lies beyond judicial cognizance. Our cases in this field seem invariably to show a discriminating analysis of the particular question posed, in terms of the history of its management by the political branches, of its susceptibility to judicial handling in the light of its nature and posture in the specific case, and of the possible consequences of judicial action. . . .

Validity of enactments: In *Coleman* v. *Miller, supra,* this Court held that the questions of how long a proposed amendment to the Federal Constitution remained open to ratification, and what effect a prior rejection had on a subsequent ratification, were committed to congressional resolution and involved criteria of decision that necessarily escaped the judicial grasp. Similar considerations apply to the enacting process: "The respect due to coequal and independent departments," and the need for finality and certainty about the status of a statute contribute to judicial reluctance to inquire whether, as passed, it complied with all requisite formalities. *Field*

v. *Clark*, 143 U.S. 649, 672, 676–677; see *Leser* v. *Garnett*, 258 U.S. 130, 137. But it is not true that courts will never delve into a legislature's records upon such a quest: If the enrolled statute lacks an effective date, a court will not hesitate to seek it in the legislative journals in order to preserve the enactment. *Gardner* v. *The Collector*, 6 Wall. 499. The political question doctrine, a tool for maintenance of governmental order, will not be so applied as to promote only disorder. . . .

It is apparent that several formulations which vary slightly according to the settings in which the questions arise may describe a political question, although each has one or more elements which identify it as essentially a function of the separation of powers. Prominent on the surface of any case held to involve a political question is found a textually demonstrable constitutional commitment of the issue to a coordinate political department; or a lack of judicially discoverable and manageable standards for resolving it; or the impossibility of deciding without an initial policy determination of a kind clearly for nonjudicial discretion; or the impossibility of a court's undertaking independent resolution without expressing lack of the respect due coordinate branches of government; or an unusual need for unquestioning adherence to a political decision already made; or the potentiality of embarrassment from multifarious pronouncements by various departments on one question.

Unless one of these formulations is inextricable from the case at bar, there should be no dismissal for nonjusticiability on the ground of a political question's presence. The doctrine of which we treat is one of "political questions," not one of "political cases." The courts cannot reject as "no law suit" a bona fide controversy as to whether some action denominated "political" exceeds constitutional authority. The cases we have reviewed show the necessity for discriminating inquiry into the precise facts and posture of the particular case, and the impossibility of resolution by any semantic cataloguing.

But it is argued that this case shares the characteristics of decisions that constitute a category not yet considered, cases concerning the Constitution's guaranty, in Art. IV, § 4, of a republican form of government. A conclusion as to whether the case at bar does present a political question cannot be confidently reached until we have considered those cases with special care. We shall discover that Guaranty Clause claims involve those elements which define a "political question," and for that reason and no other, they are nonjusticiable. In particular, we shall discover that the nonjusticiability of such claims has nothing to do with their touching upon matters of state governmental organization.

Republican form of government: Luther v. *Borden*, 7 How. 1, though in form simply an action for damages for trespass was, as Daniel Webster said in opening the argument for the defense, ''an unusual case'' [footnote deleted]. The defendants, admitting an otherwise tortious breaking and entering, sought to justify their action on the ground that they were agents of the established lawful government of Rhode Island, which State was then under martial law to defend itself from active insurrection; that the plaintiff was engaged in that insurrection; and that they entered under orders to arrest the plaintiff. The case arose ''out of the unfortunate political differences which agitated the people of Rhode Island in 1841 and 1842,'' 7 How., at 34, and which had resulted in a situation wherein two groups laid competing claims to recognition as the lawful government [footnote deleted]. . . .

. . . Having already noted the absence of standards whereby the choice between governments could be made by a court acting independently, Chief Justice Taney now found further textual and practical reasons for concluding that, if any department of the United States was empowered by the Guaranty Clause to resolve the issue, it was not the judiciary:

> Under this article of the Constitution it rests with Congress to decide what government is the established one in a State. . . .

Clearly, several factors were thought by the Court in *Luther* to make the question there ''political'': the commitment to the other branches of the decision as to which is the lawful state government; the unambiguous action by the President, in recognizing the charter government as the lawful authority; the need for finality in the executive's decision; and the lack of criteria by which a court could determine which form of government was republican [footnote deleted].

But the only significance that *Luther* could have for our immediate purposes is in its holding that the Guaranty Clause is not a repository of judicially manageable standards which a court could utilize independently in order to identify a State's lawful government. The Court has since refused to resort to the Guaranty Clause—which alone had been invoked for the purpose—as the source of a constitutional standard for invalidating state action. . . .·

Just as the Court has consistently held that a challenge to state action based on the Guaranty Clause presents no justiciable question so has it held, and for the same reasons, that challenges to congressional action on the ground of inconsistency with that clause present no justiciable question. . . .

We come, finally, to the ultimate inquiry whether our precedents as to what constitutes a nonjusticiable "political question" bring the case before us under the umbrella of that doctrine. A natural beginning is to note whether any of the common characteristics which we have been able to identify and label descriptively are present. We find none: The question here is the consistency of state action with the Federal Constitution. We have no question decided, or to be decided, by a political branch of government coequal with this Court. Nor do we risk embarrassment of our government abroad, or grave disturbance at home if we take issue with Tennessee as to the constitutionality of her action here challenged. Nor need the appellants, in order to succeed in this action, ask the Court to enter upon policy determinations for which judicially manageable standards are lacking. Judicial standards under the Equal Protection Clause are well developed and familiar, and it has been open to courts since the enactment of the Fourteenth Amendment to determine, if on the particular facts they must, that a discrimination reflects *no* policy, but simply arbitrary and capricious action.

This case does, in one sense, involve the allocation of political power within a State, and the appellants might conceivably have added a claim under the Guaranty Clause. Of course, as we have seen, any reliance on that clause would be futile. But because any reliance on the Guaranty Clause could not have succeeded it does not follow that appellants may not be heard on the equal protection claim which in fact they tender. True, it must be clear that the Fourteenth Amendment claim is not so enmeshed with those political question elements which render Guaranty Clause claims nonjusticiable as actually to present a political question itself. But we have found that not to be the case here. . . .

We conclude then that the nonjusticiability of claims resting on the Guaranty Clause which arises from their embodiment of questions that were thought "political," can have no bearing upon the justiciability of the equal protection claim presented in this case. Finally, we emphasize that it is the involvement in Guaranty Clause claims of the elements thought to define "political questions," and no other feature, which could render them nonjusticiable. Specifically, we have said that such claims are not held nonjusticiable because they touch matters of state governmental organization. . . .

We conclude that the complaint's allegations of a denial of equal protection present a justiciable constitutional cause of action upon which appellants are entitled to a trial and a decision. The right asserted is within the reach of judicial protection under the Fourteenth Amendment.

The judgment of the District Court is reversed and the cause is remanded for further proceedings consistent with this opinion.

Reversed and remanded.

8. Excerpts from Dyer v. Blair, 390 F. Supp. 1291 (S.D. Ill. 1975)

[Some footnotes have been deleted. The remaining notes have been renumbered and follow the text.]

Memorandum and Order
Stevens, Circuit Judge.

The question presented in each of these cases is whether action taken during the 78th General Assembly of the Illinois legislature constituted "ratification" of the proposed Equal Rights Amendment to the United States Constitution within the meaning of article V of that instrument. That amendment received a favorable vote of more than a majority but less than three-fifths of the members of each house of the Illinois legislature. The question arises because the precise meaning of the term "ratified" has not yet been given a federal definition, but the Illinois State Constitution, as well as a rule adopted by the Illinois House of Representatives and a ruling of the President of the Illinois Senate in the 78th General Assembly, have pre-scribed a three-fifths majority requirement for amendment to the federal Constitution.

We first more fully describe the manner in which the issue arose and identify the specific motions which are before us; we next explain why we believe the question is justiciable, notwithstanding defendants' argument that it is a "political question"; we then explain our understanding of the term "ratified" as used in article V; and finally we decide whether Illinois ratified the proposed Equal Rights Amendment during the 78th General Assembly.

Article XIV, § 4 of the Illinois Constitution of 1970 provided, for the first time, explicit procedures for the Illinois General Assembly to approve amendments to the United States Constitution:

§ 4. Amendments to the Constitution of the United States
The affirmative vote of three-fifths of the members elected to each house of the General Assembly shall be required to request Congress to call a Federal Constitutional Convention, to ratify a proposed amendment to the Constitution of the United States, or to call a State Convention to ratify a proposed amendment to the Constitution of the United States. The General Assembly shall not take action on any proposed amendment to the Constitution of the United States submitted for

ratification by legislatures unless a majority of the members of the General Assembly shall have been elected after the proposed amendment has been submitted for ratification. The requirements of this Section shall govern to the extent that they are not inconsistent with requirements established by the United States.

No action was taken on the ratification of E.R.A. by the Illinois House of Representatives during the 77th General Assembly, which expired on January 9, 1973. As Representative Juckett explained, this was in keeping with the "waiting period" provision of article XIV, § 4. On May 24, 1972, however, the Senate of the 77th General Assembly did vote on Senate Joint Resolution 62, the E.R.A. The resolution received 30 affirmative votes with 21 members opposed and one voting "present," a constitutional majority[1] of the 59 Senate members but six votes short of three-fifths. . . . An attempt . . . to amend Rule 42 to require only 89 votes, a constitutional majority, for the ratification of amendments to the federal Constitution was withdrawn and referred to the House Rules Committee.

Subsequently, on April 4, 1973, House Resolution 176, which would have amended Rule 42 in that respect, was reported favorably by the Rules Committee, but was defeated by the full House 69–90. Debate over this Resolution centered on an opinion that Illinois Attorney General William Scott had given then Speaker of the House W. Robert Blair on May 11, 1972, that article XIV, § 4 of the Illinois Constitution, insofar as it required both a three-fifths vote and a waiting period, was in conflict with articles V and VI of the federal Constitution and, consequently, of no effect.[2] Proponents of the amendment to Rule 42 relied heavily on this opinion. . . .

Thus, on April 4, 1973, Speaker W. Robert Blair ruled that a three-fifths vote would be necessary to pass the resolution ratifying E.R.A. When that vote was taken that day, House Joint Resolution 14 received 95 votes, with 72 members voting "no" and 2 "present." Consequently, E.R.A. received more than the 89 votes necessary for a constitutional majority but fewer than the 107 votes needed to reach the three-fifths requirement. Blair ruled that the resolution had failed to pass.[3]

[Subsequently four representatives brought suit alleging Article XIV, §4 of the Illinois constitution was void and could not require a three-fifths vote. They similarly questioned House Rule 42(d) and its 107-vote requirement as being in contravention of Article V of the federal Constitution. Relief sought included convening of a three-judge court, a declaratory judgment, an injunction enjoining House Speaker Blair from enforcement of the same, and a mandatory injunction directing Blair to certify passage of H.J.R.14 (ERA). The issue was declared not ripe for review since the Illinois senate had taken no action on the matter at that time. On June 18,

1974, the senate officially voted on S.J.R. 68, Senate President William Harris ruling that a three-fifths vote (36) was required for adoption, despite Senate Rule 6 (apparently adopted because of Attorney General Scott's opinion) providing for a majority vote on constitutional amendments. The resolution received 30 of 55 votes and was recorded as lost. The court took jurisdiction, noting that the problem of ripeness was cured by the senate vote.

In the intervening period, the same plaintiffs and two state senators filed a second suit similar to the first, adding the senate president as a defendant. The suit was transferred to the three-judge panel considering the first matter.

Much of the procedural maneuvering in the Illinois legislature was set against the background of opinions issued by Illinois Attorney General William Scott, discussed in this case by the Court.]

II

Defendants contend that these cases present a "political question," that is to say, a question which can only be answered by either the executive or the legislative branch of the Federal Government. The contention is supported by alternative arguments: first, that Congress has sole and complete control over the entire amending process, subject to no judicial review; and second, that even if every aspect of the amending process is not controlled by Congress, the specific issue raised in these cases is.

There is force to the first argument since it was expressly accepted by four Justices of the Supreme Court in Coleman v. Miller, 307 U.S. 433, 59 S.Ct. 972, 83 L.Ed. 1385.[4] But since a majority of the Court refused to accept that position in that case, and since the Court has on several occasions decided questions arising under article V, even in the face of "political question" contentions, that argument is not one which a District Court is free to accept. We therefore must consider whether this particular issue is a "political question" under the standards identified in cases such as Powell v. McCormack, 395 U.S. 486, 518–519; 89 S.Ct. 1944, 23 L.Ed.2d 491, and Baker v. Carr, 369 U.S. 186, 217, 82 S.Ct. 691, 7 L.Ed.2d 663, and in Chief Justice Hughes' opinion for the Court in Coleman v. Miller, supra.

The text of the Constitution does not expressly direct Congress, rather than the judiciary, to interpret the word "ratified" as it is used in article V, or to decide whether a particular state has taken action which constitutes ratification of a proposed amendment. Rather than relying on the "textual commitment" test for identifying a political question, defendants primarily suggest that the issue is one which may produce an unseemly conflict between coordinate branches of government unless we treat it as nonjusticiable.[5] We are persuaded, however, that this suggestion is foreclosed by the Supreme Court's rejection of a comparable argument in Powell v. McCormack, *supra*.

In that case the Court was requested to pass on the constitutionality of the refusal by the House of Representatives to seat the plaintiff, who had been duly elected from the Eighteenth Congressional District of New York to serve in the 90th Congress. The refusal was not based on the plaintiff's failure to meet the requirements of age, citizenship and residence contained in article I, § 2 of the Constitution. The question whether the House could refuse to seat an elected representative on any ground presented, quite obviously, a far more dramatic potential for conflict between coordinate branches than does the question involved in this case. In the *Powell* case, after concluding that the "textual commitment" formulation of the political question doctrine did not bar federal courts from adjudicating the plaintiff's claim, the Court discussed other considerations as follows:

> Respondents' alternate contention is that the case presents a political question because judicial resolution of petitioners' claim would produce a "potentially embarrassing confrontation between coordinate branches" of the Federal Government. But, as our interpretation of Art. I, § 5, discloses, a determination of petitioner Powell's right to sit would require no more than an interpretation of the Constitution. Such a determination falls within the traditional role accorded courts to interpret the law, and does not involve a "lack of the respect due [a] coordinate [branch] of government," nor does it involve an "initial policy determination of a kind clearly for nonjudicial discretion." Baker v. Carr, 369 U.S. 186, at 217, 82 S.Ct. 691, at 710 [7 L.Ed.2d 663]. Our system of government requires that federal courts on occasion interpret the Constitution in a manner at variance with the construction given the document by another branch. The alleged conflict that such an adjudication may cause cannot justify the courts' avoiding their constitutional responsibility. . . .
>
> Nor are any of the other formulations of a political question "inextricable from the case at bar." Baker v. Carr, *supra* [369 U.S.] at 217, 82 S.Ct. [691] at 710. Petitioners seek a determination that the House was without power to exclude Powell from the 90th Congress, which, we have seen, requires an interpretation of the Constitution—a determination for which clearly there are "judicially . . . manageable standards." Finally, a judicial resolution of petitioners' claim will not result in "multifarious pronouncements by various departments on one question." For, as we noted in Baker v. Carr, *supra*, at 211, 82 S.Ct. [691], at 706 it is the responsibility of this Court to act as the ultimate interpreter of the Constitution. Marbury v. Madison, 1 Cranch (5 U.S.) 137, 2 L.Ed. 60 (1803). Thus, we conclude that petitioners' claim is not barred by the political question doctrine, and having determined that the claim is otherwise generally justiciable, we hold that the case is justiciable.

395 U.S. at 548–549, 89 S.Ct. at 1978 (footnote omitted).

The Court's reasoning in Powell v. McCormack requires a similar conclusion in this case. Decision of the question presented requires no more than an interpretation of the Constitution. Such a decision falls squarely within the traditional role of the federal judiciary to construe that document.[6] The possibility that such an adjudication may conflict with the views of Congress cannot justify the courts' avoiding their constitutional responsibility. As the Supreme Court pointedly noted in its citation of McPherson v. Blacker, 146 U.S. 1, 24, 13 S.Ct. 3, 36 L.Ed. 869, the possibility that action might be taken in disregard of a final judicial determination is an "inadmissible suggestion."

The strongest argument for regarding the issue presented by these cases as a "political question" rests on an asserted "lack of judicially discoverable and manageable standards for resolving it." *See* Baker v. Carr, 369 U.S. at 217, 82 S.Ct. at 710. That argument is buttressed by the holding in Coleman v. Miller, 307 U.S. 433, 59 S.Ct. 972, 83 L.Ed. 1385 that the question whether the lapse of 13 years between the proposal of an amendment and the favorable action by the Kansas legislature made the ratification ineffective was a "political question" to be finally determined by Congress.[7]

That holding was based on the absence of any acceptable criteria for making a judicial determination of whether the proposed amendment had lost its vitality through lapse of time. The Court noted that different periods might be reasonable for different proposed amendments and that varying economic or social conditions might support differing conclusions. Such considerations, although entirely acceptable as a predicate for decision by political departments of the government, might be wholly inappropriate as a basis for judicial decision.[8]

Although the issue in these cases is somewhat comparable to the lapse of time issue in *Coleman* in that the criteria for judicial determination are, perhaps, equally hard to find, the answer does not depend on economic, social or political factors that vary from time to time and might well change during the interval between the proposal and ratification. A question that might be answered in different ways for different amendments must surely be controlled by political standards rather than standards easily characterized as judicially manageable.

It is primarily the character of the standards, not merely the difficulty of their application, that differentiates between those which are political and those which are judicial. The mere fact that a court has little or nothing but the language of the Constitution as a guide to its interpretation does not mean that the task of construction is judicially unmanageable. . . .

We are persuaded that the word "ratification" as used in article V of the federal Constitution must be interpreted with the kind of consistency that is characteristic of judicial, as opposed to political, decision making. We conclude, therefore, that whatever the word "ratification" means as it is used in article V, that meaning must be constant for each amendment that Congress may propose. We turn, then, to the problem of ascertaining the meaning of that term.

III

The power of a state legislature to ratify an amendment to the federal Constitution is derived from that instrument. By virtue of the supremacy clause in article VI,[9] it is clear that the legislature's ratifying function may not be abridged by a state. Mr. Justice Brandeis, speaking for a unanimous court in Leser v. Garnett, 258 U.S. 130, 42 S.Ct. 217, 66 L.Ed. 505, made this point abundantly clear.

> The second contention is that in the Constitutions of several of the 36 states named in the proclamation of the Secretary of State there are provisions which render inoperative the alleged ratifications by their Legislatures. The argument is that by reason of the specific provisions the legislatures were without power to ratify. But the function of a state Legislature in ratifying a proposed amendment to the federal Constitution, like the function of Congress in proposing the amendment, is a federal function derived from the federal Constitution; and it transcends any limitations sought to be imposed by the people of a state. Hawke v. Smith, No. 1, 253 U.S. 221, 40 S.Ct. 495, 64 L.Ed. 871; Hawke v. Smith, No. 2, 253 U.S. 231, 40 S.Ct. 498, 64 L.Ed. 877; National Prohibition Cases, 253 U.S. 350, 386, 40 S.Ct. 486, 588, 64 L.Ed. 946.

258 U.S. at 136–137, 42 S.Ct. at 217.

Quite clearly, therefore, if the federal Constitution specifies that ratification shall be accomplished in a particular way, or by a particular vote of a state legislature or a state convention, no state may superimpose a more stringent requirement on that federal specification. The difficulty presented by the cases before us, however, results from the fact that neither the Constitution itself, nor the record of the deliberations of the constitutional convention which drafted it, contains any unambiguous description or definition of what the state legislature must do in order to perform its federal ratifying function.

History teaches us that the framers of the Constitution were dissatisfied with the extraordinary difficulty of amending the Articles of Confederation.[10] Accordingly, there was extensive discussion and debate about article V of the new Constitution, but it is fair to state that such deliberation was concerned almost exclusively with the procedure for initiating proposed amendments, or with the number of states which must express their assent to a proposal in order to make it effective. We have found no evidence of any significant discussion about the procedure which a state legislature or state convention should follow in deciding whether or not to ratify a proposal.

Congress is, of course, given the power to decide whether the ratifying process should be performed by state conventions or by state legislatures, and the Supreme Court has affirmed Congress' power to prescribe a time limit within which the ratifying process must be completed. But the Constitution is totally silent with respect to the procedure which each state convention or each state legislature, as the case may be, should follow in performing its ratifying function.

There can be no doubt about the fact that the Constitution permits many aspects of the ratification procedure to be determined by representatives of the several states. As Professor Dodd has noted:

> It should be remembered, however, that ratification is by state legislatures, and that although the state may not provide any other method of ratification or impose limitations upon the power to ratify, it does seem to be clearly within the power of the state through its constitution or otherwise to determine what shall be the organization of the state's representative legislative body, and what shall be the quorum for action by that body. It, of course, also rests within the power of the state itself as to when regular or special sessions of the state's representative body shall meet, and as to how that representative body shall be organized.

Dodd, Amending the Federal Constitution, 30 Yale L.J. 321, 344–345 (1921).[11]

Arguably, the vote required to effectuate a ratification might be considered a procedural matter, comparable to the determination of a quorum, subject to control by the states. Alternatively, it can be argued with equal force that since the term must have a federal definition, and since the number of votes required to ratify is a matter of critical importance, that number must be set by federal law. Theoretically, the number might be determined by at least five different standards.

First, since the entire ratification process is not effective unless three-fourths of the state legislatures have concurred, it might be inferred that a comparable fraction of each body must support a ratifying resolution. Second, it might be thought that a lesser extraordinary majority—such as the Illinois three-fifths requirement—of the legislators elected and eligible to vote would be appropriate. Or, third, an extraordinary majority of the legislators present and voting could be required. Conceivably this latter extraordinary majority might be obtained more easily than the fourth alternative, a vote of 51% of the elected legislators, a constitutional majority.

And fifth, as plaintiffs argue in this case, a simple majority, a majority of a quorum—or more precisely of the legislators present when a quorum is present—may suffice.[12]

The vote of the Kansas Legislature, which under the holding in Coleman v. Miller, 307 U.S. 433, 59 S.Ct. 972, 83 L.Ed. 1385, constituted an effective ratification, was 21 to 20. We may take it as decided, therefore, that an extraordinary majority is not *required* by federal law.[13] There is, moreover, some evidence that when article V was drafted the framers assumed that state legislatures would act by majority vote.[14] That evidence, like the text of article V itself, is equally consistent with the view that a majority of a quorum would be sufficient, or with a view that a majority of the elected legislators would be required. And, of course, it is also consistent with the view that the framers did not intend to impose either of those alternatives upon the state legislators, but, instead, intended to leave that choice to the ratifying assemblies.

This last view seems most plausible to us. If the framers had intended to require the state legislatures to act by simple majority, we think they would have said so explicitly. When the Constitution requires action to be taken by an extraordinary majority, that requirement is plainly stated.[15] While the omission of a comparable requirement in connection with ratification makes it quite clear that a bare majority is permissible, it does not necessarily indicate that either a simple majority or a constitutional majority must be accepted as necessary. We think the omission more reasonably indicates that the framers intended to treat the determination of the vote required to pass a ratifying resolution as an aspect of the process that each state legislature, or state convention, may specify for itself.

This conclusion is consistent with—though by no means compelled by—the underlying philosophy of the framers with regard to the respective roles of the central government and the several state governments. Madison expressed the thought in urging ratification of the Constitution in The Federalist No. 45:

> The powers delegated by the proposed Constitution to the federal government are few and defined. Those which are to remain in the State governments are numerous and indefinite.

The Federalist No. 45, at 303 (Modern Library ed.) (Madison). The ratifying power did not, of course, "remain in the State governments" because it was created by article V of the new Constitution. But the failure to prescribe any particular ratification procedure, or required vote to effectuate a ratification, is certainly consistent with the basic understanding that state legislatures should have the power and the discretion to determine for themselves how they should discharge the responsibilities committed to them by the federal government.[16]

In addition, were we to conclude that article V does mandate a particular majority vote in each state legislature, we would then have to choose among the myriad of possibilities set forth above. The fact that the several states have actually adopted a wide variety of ratification requirements (*see* n. 34, *supra*) demonstrates that no one voting percentage or procedure is manifestly preferable to all others. Moreover, this history manifests a common understanding that there is no federal objection to the state legislatures' independent determination of their own voting requirements. The absence of criticism of this independent action throughout our history strongly suggests that the common understanding existed when the original Constitution was ratified and that the framers did not intend to prescribe any one of the various alternatives as mandatory.

Plaintiffs in the cases before us have argued that ratification under article V requires the use of a simple majority, or, at most, a majority of those entitled to vote, a constitutional majority. We find no principled reason for holding that either of those procedures, rather than any of the supermajority hybrids that have emerged since article V was adopted, is the one mandated by the Constitution.

Article V identifies the body—either a legislature or a convention— which must ratify a proposed amendment. The act of ratification is an expression of consent to the amendment by that body. By what means that body shall decide to consent or not to consent is a matter for that body to determine for itself. This conclusion is not inconsistent with the premise that the definition of the term "ratified" is a matter of federal law. The term merely requires that the decision to consent or not to consent to a proposed amendment be made by each legislature, or by each convention, in accordance with procedures which each such body shall prescribe.[17]

IV

The Supreme Court has held that a state may not inhibit its legislature's federal power to ratify a proposed amendment to the United States Constitution by requiring approval at a popular referendum;[18] it seems equally clear that a state constitution may not require that a new legislature be elected before the proposal may be considered.[19] The Illinois Attorney General has on three occasions expressed the opinion that a due regard for the federal character of the legislature's ratifying function must invalidate the Illinois constitutional requirement of a favorable vote by a three-fifths majority. *See* nn. 5, 8, *supra*.

The Attorney General's analysis is consistent with ours. We have concluded that article V delegates to the state legislatures—or the state conventions depending upon the mode of ratification selected by Congress—the power to determine their own voting requirements. The decisions of the Supreme Court, as well as the text of article V, illuminate the critical point that the delegation is not to the states but rather to the designated ratifying bodies. We do not believe that delegated federal power may be inhibited by a state constitutional provision which, in practical effect, determines whether votes of legislators opposing an amendment shall be given greater, lesser, or the same weight as the votes of legislators who favor the proposal.

In the 77th General Assembly the Illinois Senate took the position that, in the performance of its federal function, it was not inhibited by article XIV, § 4 of the Illinois Constitution and formally recorded its favorable action on the proposed Equal Rights Amendment, notwithstanding the failure to obtain a three-fifths vote. In the 78th General Assembly, however, the House as well as the Senate took a different view. If our analysis of the nature of the delegated power is correct, the Illinois constitutional provision may only be precatory in its effect on the federal process, and those bodies are free to accept or to reject the three-fifths requirement.

They did accept that requirement during the 78th General Assembly. Whether they did so because of a mistaken understanding of the applicable law (notwithstanding the advice of the Attorney General of the state that they were free to disregard the limitation), or because of their decision to respect a policy choice made by the framers of their own constitution in 1970, or simply because they independently determined that the supermajority requirement would be desirable, is of no legal significance. It is clearly not our province to inquire into the individual motives of the legislators who voted in favor of the procedural rules adopted by each branch of the General Assembly to govern its own deliberations, including those relating to ratification of a proposed amendment to the federal Constitution.[20]

In sum, we conclude that the action taken by the 78th Session of the Illinois General Assembly did not constitute an effective ratification because the resolution did not pass by the vote required by the applicable rules of procedure adopted by both houses of the legislature. This conclusion does not reflect disagreement with the contention of the plaintiffs, or the thrice-expressed opinion of the Attorney General of Illinois, that article XIV, § 4 of the Illinois Constitution of 1970 does not impose a valid restraint on the power of any session of the Illinois General Assembly to determine for itself the number of affirmative votes which will be required to ratify a proposed amendment to the Constitution of the United States.

The motions which are pending and undecided would not dispose of the entire litigation. It is apparent, however, that the record is now complete and no useful purpose would be served by further proceedings. Moreover, we are satisfied that further briefing of the legal issue would not modify the conclusion to which our research has led us. It therefore seems appropriate to enter final judgment disposing of the entire litigation.

The three-judge court was convened in each of these cases because each complaint prayed for the entry of an injunction commanding state officials to take certain action predicated on the assumption that the Illinois legislature has effectively ratified the Equal Rights Amendment. We have concluded that plaintiffs are not entitled to such injunctive relief. The reasoning which led us to that conclusion has required us to express an opinion concerning the legal import, or lack thereof, of article XIV, § 4 of the Illinois Constitution. Since the ultimate decision of the controversy between the parties is controlled by the legislature's procedural rules, and, in final analysis, would be unaffected by the entry of a declaratory judgment declaring article XIV, § 4 invalid, such a judgment would be merely advisory in character and therefore beyond our power to enter. Accordingly, we deny (1) the motion for summary declaratory judgment on Count I of the *Dyer* Complaint; (2) the Motion for Partial Summary Declaratory Judgment on Count I of the *Netsch* Complaint; and (3) the Motion for Expedited Consideration of the Motion for Partial Summary Judgment in the *Netsch* case. Finally, having determined that plaintiffs are not entitled to injunctive relief, we order that summary judgment be entered for defendants in both cases.

Notes

1. Defendants describe a "constitutional majority" as a majority of the members elected to the respective house and entitled to vote. This is in contrast to a "simple majority"—a majority of those present and voting on the measure—and an "extraordinary majority" which requires some higher percentage of the elected members to pass a question. The three-fifths requirement in article XIV, § 4 is, thus, an extraordinary majority.

2. Op. Ill. Att'y Gen. No. S–456 (1972). Attorney General Scott subsequently reiterated his conclusion that article XIV, § 4 of the Illinois Constitution was of no effect in his opinion of April 2, 1973, to W. Robert

Blair (Op. Ill. Att'y Gen. No. S–571 (1973). He also concluded that Ill. Rev. Stat. 1971, ch. 7½, § 12 (Act of June 25, 1963, Laws 1963, p. 1215. § 1), which requires a favorable vote of a constitutional majority of each house to ratify a proposed federal Constitutional amendment, was in conflict with articles V and VI of the United States Constitution, since in enacting the act the legislature had acted in its state legislative rather than its federal amendment ratification capacity. Scott did conclude, however, that "barring the use of extreme standards patently in conflict with article V, each house may, by its own rules, determine how many votes are needed to ratify a proposed amendment to the United States Constitution." Op. Ill. Att'y Gen. No. S-571 (1973).

 3. Journal of the Illinois House of Representatives 777–778 (1973).

 4. The concurring opinion by Mr. Justice Black was joined by Justices Roberts, Frankfurter and Douglas. *See* 307 U.S. at 456, 59 S.Ct. 972. Justice Black concluded his opinion as follows:

> The process itself is "political" in its entirety, from submission until an amendment becomes part of the Constitution, and is not subject to judicial guidance, control or interference at any point.
>
> Since Congress has sole and complete control over the amending process, subject to no judicial review, the views of any court upon this process cannot be binding upon Congress, and insofar as Dillon v. Gloss [256 U.S. 368, 41 S.Ct. 510, 65 L.Ed. 994] attempts judicially to impose a limitation upon the right of Congress to determine final adoption of an amendment, it should be disapproved. If Congressional determination that an amendment has been completed and become a part of the Constitution is final and removed from examination by the courts, as the Court's present opinion recognizes, surely the steps leading to that condition must be subject to the scrutiny, control and appraisal of none save the Congress, the body having exclusive power to make that final determination.
>
> Congress, possessing exclusive power over the amending process, cannot be bound by and is under no duty to accept the pronouncements upon that exclusive power by this Court or by the Kansas courts. Neither State nor Federal courts can review that power. Therefore, any judicial expression amounting to more than mere acknowledgment of exclusive Congressional power over the political process of amendment is a mere admonition to the Congress in the nature of an advisory opinion, given wholly without constitutional authority. 307 U.S. at 459–460, 59 S.Ct. at 984.

Dicta in Luther v. Borden. 48 U.S. (7 How.) 1, 39, 12 L.Ed. 581, has been read to support Justice Black's position. *See* Clark, The Supreme Court and the Amending Process, 39 Va.L.Rev. 621, 630 (1953). However, as we read the passage in question, the Court was focusing its attention on the process of amending state constitutions, rather than the federal Constitution.

 5. They point to the danger of setting the federal judiciary and the

federal and state legislatures "at constitutional loggerheads." Brief in Support of Motion to Dismiss in *Dyer* at p. 11. Any suggestion that the federal judiciary must avoid potential conflict with state legislatures over the proper interpretation of the federal Constitution is answered by the supremacy clause, article VI, cl. 2, and cases such as Gibbons v. Ogden, 22 U.S. (9 Wheat.) 1, 6 L.Ed. 23, and Baker v. Carr, 369 U.S. 186, 82 S.Ct. 691, 7 L.Ed.2d 663.

6. Although the Court will treat a certification by a legislature that it has followed a prescribed procedure in the enactment of a bill into law as conclusively determining the facts certified. Field v. Clark, 143 U.S. 649, 12 S.Ct. 495, 36 L.Ed. 294, the question whether the procedure followed by Congress was the one prescribed by the Constitution is a question the Court will answer. *See* the first two conclusions announced in the National Prohibition Cases, 253 U.S. 350, 386, 40 S.Ct. 486, 64 L. Ed. 946.

7. In *Coleman* the Court also held that the question whether the ratification of a proposed amendment was effective notwithstanding a prior rejection by the Kansas legislature was a political question. The characterization of that question as political rested largely on historic precedent. The issue had previously been considered by Congress; the Supreme Court found no basis for judicial interference with a continuation of that procedure for resolving that issue.

> We think that in accordance with this historic precedent the question of the efficacy of ratifications by state legislatures, in the light of previous rejection or attempted withdrawal, should be regarded as a political question pertaining to the political departments, with the ultimate authority in the Congress in the exercise of its control over the promulgation of the adoption of the amendment.

307 U.S. at 450, 59 S.Ct. at 981.

That reasoning does not apply to the question presented in these cases. For we have found no historic precedent indicating that Congress has previously considered a claim that a state legislature had effectively ratified a proposed amendment notwithstanding a failure to obtain the favorable vote required by its own rules of procedure.

8. "Where are to be found the criteria for such a judicial determination? None are to be found in Constitution or statute. . . . In short, the question of a reasonable time in many cases would involve, as in this case it does involve, an appraisal of a great variety of relevant conditions, political, social and economic, which can hardly be said to be within the appropriate range of evidence receivable in a court of justice and as to which it would be an extravagant extension of judicial authority to assert judicial notice as the

basis of deciding a controversy with respect to the validity of an amendment actually ratified. On the other hand, these conditions are appropriate for the consideration of the political departments of the Government. The questions they involve are essentially political and not justiciable. They can be decided by the Congress with the full knowledge and appreciation ascribed to the national legislature of the political, social and economic conditions which have prevailed during the period since the submission of the amendment.'' 307 U.S. at 453–454, 59 S.Ct. at 981.

9. "This Constitution, and the laws of the United States which shall be made in Pursuance thereof; and all Treaties made, or which shall be made, under the Authority of the United States, shall be the supreme Law of the Land; and the Judges, in every State shall be bound thereby, any Thing in the Constitution or Laws of any State to the Contrary notwithstanding.'' Article VI, clause 2.

10. Article XIII of the Articles of Confederation provided for amendment whenever it shall ''be agreed to in a Congress of the United States, and be afterwards affirmed by the Legislatures of every State.''

11. At page 65 of his treatise, The Amending of the Federal Constitution (1971), Professor Orfield made a similar observation:

> As a minimum power the state could provide for the time and place of meeting of the legislature, whether it should be bicameral or unicameral, the number and election of its members, its organization and officers. The state could perhaps even abolish its legislature altogether, at least as far as Article Five is concerned, although such action might be regarded as a failure to maintain a republican form of government.

12. Professor Orfield notes: ''Perhaps a simple majority of a quorum of each House is sufficient.'' Orfield, *supra* n. 33, at 66.

In addition, if the state legislature should decide to meet in joint session to consider the proposed amendment, numerous other possible standards, ranging from a simple majority of all members present to highly complex formulae designed to ensure that an amendment is not ratified solely on the votes of the members of one of the houses, present themselves.

A survey of the ratification majorities required by the states to adopt federal constitutional amendments, prepared by the Illinois Legislative Council, has been supplied us by the defendants. It reports that 24 states require a majority of the elected representatives (a constitutional majority); 17 states require a majority of those present and voting (a simple majority); 3 states require a majority of those elected to the state senate and two-thirds of those elected to the state house of representatives; 2 states require two-fifths of the members elected and a majority of those voting; Louisiana requires a majority of those elected to the state senate and a majority of those present and voting in the state house; Tennessee requires a majority of the authorized membership of each house notwithstanding the possible existence of vacancies; Idaho requires two-thirds of those elected.

13. The fact that an extraordinary majority is not required does not, of course, indicate that such a majority may not be permitted. Moreover, the fact that there is no constitutional impediment to the utilization by the states of extraordinary majorities for various other purposes, such as the approval of bonded indebtedness, etc., as the cases cited by amici curiae hold (*see, e.g.,* Gordon v. Lance, 403 U.S. 1, 91 S.Ct. 1889, 29 L.Ed.2d 273; Brenner v. School District of Kansas City, Mo., 403 U.S. 913, 91 S.Ct. 2225, 29 L.Ed. 2d 692), does not shed any light on the permissibility of such a requirement in connection with the performance by a state legislature of its federal ratifying function.

14. For example, during the Virginia Ratifying Convention Patrick Henry argued:

> [B]ut what is destructive and mischievous, is, that three fourths of the state legislatures, or of the state conventions must concur in the amendments when proposed! In such numerous bodies, there must necessarily be some designing, bad men. To suppose that so large a number as three fourths of the states will concur, is to suppose that they will possess genius intelligence, and integrity, approaching to miraculous. It would indeed be miraculous that they should concur in the same amendments, or even in such as would bear some likeness to one another: or four of the smallest states, that do not collectively contain one tenth part of the population of the United States, may obstruct the most salutary and necessary amendments. Nay, in these four states six tenths of the people may reject these amendments. . . . A bare majority in these four small states may hinder the adoption of amendments.

Quoted in III J. Elliot, *supra*, n. 29 at 49–50.

Similarly, during the debates in the House on the proposed Bill of Rights, Representative Tucker remarked:

> I conceived it difficult, if not impossible, to obtain essential amendments by the way pointed out in the constitution. . . . It will be found, I fear, still more difficult than I apprehended; for perhaps these amendments . . . will be submitted for ratification to the Legislatures of the several States, instead of State conventions, in which case the chance is still worse. The Legislatures of almost all the States consist of two independent, distinct bodies; the amendments must be adopted by three-fourths of such Legislatures; that is to say, they must meet the approbation of the majority of each of eighteen deliberative assemblies.

Quoted in 2 B. Schwartz, The Bill of Rights: A Documentary History 1115 (1971).

15. Two-thirds of the members present in the Senate are required to convict in an impeachment proceeding (art. I, § 3). Two-thirds of the members of the House or Senate are required to expel a member (art. 1, § 5). Two-thirds of the members of each house are necessary to override a Presidential veto (art. I, § 7). Two-thirds of the members of the Senate concur in the making of all treaties (art. II, § 2). Two-thirds of both houses are needed to propose constitutional amendments, and the legislatures or conventions of three-fourths of the states must ratify such (art. V). If a Presidential election is decided in the House of Representatives, a quorum consists of a member or members from two-thirds of the states (amend. 12). Similarly, two-thirds of the members of the Senate constitute a quorum for the selection of a Vice-President (*id.*). A vote of two-thirds of each house may remove the disability imposed on persons having engaged in rebellion or insurrection (amend. 14, § 3). A two-thirds vote of both houses is required to determine that the President continues to be unable to discharge the powers and duties of his office (amend. 25).

16. At the time the framers inserted the provision empowering the legislatures of two-thirds of the states to apply to Congress for the calling of a convention to propose amendments, James Madison noted that no mention was made of the procedures that would govern the activities of such a convention. ''[D]ifficulties might arise as to the form, the quorum, &c, which in constitutional regulations ought to be as much as possible avoided.'' V. J. Elliot, *supra*, at 551. Nevertheless, no change in the language of article V was made; presumably, such procedural matters were left to be determined by such a convention itself.

17. This is not to suggest that we would entertain a cause of action attacking a state ratification certification on the grounds that the legislature had failed to comply with its own procedures. As the Court stated in Leser v. Garnett, 258 U.S. 130, 137, 42 S.Ct. 217, 218, 66 L.Ed. 505:

> As the legislatures of Tennessee and of West Virginia had power to adopt the resolutions of ratification, official notice to the Secretary [of State], duly authenticated, that they had done so, was conclusive upon him, and, being certified to by his proclamation, is conclusive upon the courts.

18. Hawke v. Smith (No. 1), 253 U.S. 221, 40 S.Ct. 495, 64 L.Ed. 871; National Prohibition Cases, 253 U.S. 350, 40 S.Ct. 486, 64 L.Ed. 946.

19. Indeed, such a provision in the Tennessee Constitution was held unconstitutional in Leser v. Garnett, 258 U.S. 130, 136–137, 42 S.Ct. 217, 66 L.Ed. 505. One of the unenumerated state constitutional provisions at issue therein was that of Tennessee. *See* Leser v. Garnett, 139 Md. 46, 114 A. 840, 846–847 (1921).

20. *See* Palmer v. Thompson, 403 U.S. 217, 224–225, 91 S.Ct. 1940, 29 L.Ed.2d 438; United States v. O'Brien, 391 U.S. 367, 382–384, 88 S.Ct. 1673, 20 L.Ed.2d 672; Fletcher v. Peck, 10 U.S. (6 Cranch) 87, 130, 3 L.Ed. 162.

9. Excerpts from Opinions by the Attorney General of Illinois

The elevation of Judge Stevens to the Supreme Court after the decision in *Dyer* v. *Blair* gives added interest to the narrowly defined procedural issues in that case. Since the fine procedural lines drawn by the opinions of Illinois Attorney General William Scott were cited with apparent approval by now Justice Stevens in *Dyer*, the decision in *Dyer* should be read with the caveat that extending the logic of the case beyond its strictly construed facts might lead to unwarranted conclusions.

a. NO. S-455 *OP. ATT'Y. GEN.* 104 (1972).

Your questions relate to restrictions placed on the power of the General Assembly to ratify a proposed amendment to the United States Constitution. There are two such restrictions found in section 4 of article XIV of the Illinois Constitution of 1970:

> (1) Action on a proposed amendment to the United States Constitution must be delayed until a majority of the legislature has been elected after the amendment is submitted to the state for ratification.
> (2) An affirmative vote of three-fifths of the members of each house of the General Assembly is necessary to ratify a proposed amendment to the United States Constitution.

The issue thus is one of power. Can the people of the State of Illinois, through their State Constitution, restrict or regulate the ratification of amendments to the United States Constitution by the General Assembly.

The Federal Constitution is primarily a grant of power whereas a State Constitution is not a grant, but is a limitation, of power. . . .

The power of the people of a state, through their State Constitution, to regulate the method by which an amendment to the United States Constitution can be ratified was the main issue of *Hawke* v. *Smith*, 253 U.S. 221. . . .

Hawke v. *Smith, supra*, holds that the people of the United States, in ratifying the United States Constitution, relinquished certain powers; specifically, the power to control the amending process of the United States Constitution. They delegated to Congress the power to propose amendments to the United States Constitution and to choose the method of ratification of proposed amendments, i.e., state legislatures or state conventions. Once the state legislature is chosen by Congress as the method of ratification, said legislatures have the power, delegated by the people of the United States, to ratify or reject said proposed amendments. As Mr. Justice Day pointed out in his opinion, the people of the United States could have reserved to themselves the power to ratify United States constitutional amendments but they chose instead the method outlined in article V. (*Hawke* v. *Smith*, 253 U.S. 221.) Thus, we have emerging via *Hawke* v. *Smith, supra*, the notion that the legislature, when ratifying a proposed amendment to the United States Constitution, is carrying out a federal function wholly unrelated to state legislative functions. The legislature, when ratifying a proposed amendment, is not subject to regulation or restriction by the people of the state.

Edward J. Brundage, Attorney General of the State of Illinois (1917–1924) recognized that the people of the State of Illinois did not have the power to place restrictions on the legislature's ratification of proposed amendments. See, 1919–1920 Ill. Att. Gen. Op. 972.

Charles E. Woodward, President, Constitutional Convention of 1920, wrote to Attorney General Brundage asking his opinion on the constitutionality of proposal No. 382, which read as follows:

> Whenever the Congress of the United States shall by appropriate resolution propose an amendment to the Federal Constitution, such resolution shall be filed and remain in the office of the Governor until after the members of the next General Assembly shall have been elected.
>
> When pursuant to law and this election, the General Assembly shall have been organized, the Governor shall present such resolution and proposed amendment for consideration.

Even delegates to the recent Illinois Constitutional Convention (Sixth Illinois Constitutional Convention) had their misgivings about the constitutionality of delaying action on a proposed amendment until a new legislature is elected. (See, 6th Ill. Const. Convention, Verbatim Transcript, No. 29, March 26, 1970, p. 167). Likewise, the Committee on Style and Drafting placed the last sentence into section 4 of article XIV of the Illinois Constitution of 1970 because that committee was aware of the strong possibility that portions of section 4 would conflict with federal law. The last sentence of section 4 bears repeating at this time:

The requirements of this Section shall govern to the extent that they are not inconsistent with requirements established by the United States.

b. NO. S-571 *OP. ATT'Y. GEN.* 36 (1973).

On May 11, 1972, . . . I held that certain provisions of section 4 of article XIV of the Illinois Constitution of 1970 that attempted to restrict the powers of the General Assembly to ratify a proposed amendment to the United States Constitution were in conflict with article V of the United States Constitution. . . . I stated as follows:

I am of the opinion that the second sentence of section 4 of Article XIV of the Illinois Constitution of 1970 which requires a delay in consideration of the proposed twenty-seventh amendment to the United States Constitution (the "Women's rights" Amendment) is contrary to Article V of the United States Constitution.

. . . The function of a state legislature in ratifying a proposed amendment to the Federal Constitution, like the function of Congress in proposing the amendment, is a federal function derived from the Federal Constitution; and it transcends any limitations sought to be imposed by the people of a state." (*Leser* v. *Garnett*, 258 U.S. 130, 137). This principle and the principles of law enunciated in *Hawke* v. *Smith*, 253 U.S. 221, necessitate the further conclusion that the requirement of a three-fifths vote of each house of the General Assembly to ratify is also contrary to the federal constitution.

Please note that the requirement of an affirmative vote of three-fifths of the members of each house of the General Assembly to ratify a proposed amendment to the United States Constitution is declared to be unconstitutional and, therefore, is void.

Now, you ask what number of votes by the members of each house of the General Assembly is needed to ratify a proposed amendment to the United States Constitution.

Section 1 of "AN ACT in relation to ratification of proposed amendments to the Constitution of the United States of America" (Ill. Rev. Stat. 1971, ch. 7½ par. 12) was enacted by the 73rd General Assembly on April 25, 1963 (S.B. 16) and was approved by the Governor on June 25, 1963. (Laws of 1963, p. 1215.) Said section 1 reads as follows:

Whenever the Congress of the United States of America has adopted a proposal to amend the Constitution of the United States of America and the mode of ratification thereof prescribed by Congress is by the legislatures of the several states, a joint resolution proposing the ratification of such proposed amendment shall be considered by both houses of the General Assembly of this State. Such joint resolution to ratify the Congressional proposition to amend the Constitution of the United States shall be validly adopted by the General Assembly of this State only if it receives the favorable vote of a constitutional majority of the members of each house of the General Assembly.

Note that section 1 requires a favorable vote of a constitutional majority of the members of each house of the General Assembly to ratify a proposed amendment to the United States Constitution. A majority of the members elected to each house of the General Assembly constitutes a constitutional majority. See, Ill. Const., art. IV, sec. 12 [1870]; Ill. Const., art. IV, sec. 8(c).

The reasons that led me to declare the aforementioned provisions of section 4, article XIV to be unconstitutional also compel me to declare section 1 of "AN ACT in relation to ratification of proposed amendments to the Constitution of the United States of America" . . . to be unconstitutional. Said section 1 with its requirement of a constitutional majority under the Illinois Constitution is in conflict with article V of the United States Constitution and therefore is void.

We must once again be reminded that the People of the United States in ratifying the United States Constitution relinquished certain powers; specifically, they relinquished the power to control the process by which the United States Constitution is amended. They delegated to Congress the power to propose amendments to the United States Constitution and to choose the method of ratification of the proposed amendments, i.e., State legislatures or State conventions. Once the State legislature is chosen by Congress as the method of ratification, said legislatures have the power, delegated by the People of the United States, to ratify or reject said proposed amendments. The People of the United States could have reserved to themselves the power to ratify United States constitutional amendments but they chose instead the method outlined in article V. Thus, the legislature, when ratifying a proposed amendment to the United States Constitution is carrying out a Federal function unrelated to its State legislative function; it is acting in a Federal capacity, deriving its powers from article V of the United States Constitution. The legislature, when ratifying a proposed amendment to the United States Constitution, is not subject to regulation or restriction by the People of the State through State constitutional enactment or by the State legislature itself acting in a purely State capacity.

In considering whether the Illinois legislature in its adoption of section 1 of "AN ACT in relation to ratification of proposed amendments to the Constitution of the United States of America" . . . was acting as an instrumentality of the Federal amending process under article V, on the one hand, or acting on behalf of the People of the State of Illinois, on the other, it is necessary to briefly examine the character of the legislature as well as certain attributes of the Act here in question. In its usual and customary functions, the Illinois General Assembly represents the People of the State of Illinois. The legislative power of the People of the State of Illinois is vested in the General Assembly. (Ill. Const., art. IV, sec. 1.) Since a State Constitution is generally construed as a limitation on the powers of the General Assembly, all the powers not specifically denied the General Assembly in the State Constitution reside in the General Assembly. . . .

. . . [T]he 73rd General Assembly was acting in a State legislative capacity when it enacted section 1 of "AN ACT in relation to ratification of proposed amendments to the Constitution of the United States", (Ill. Rev. Stat. 1971, ch. 7½, par. 12.) However, as I have stated earlier, the General Assembly, in its State legislative capacity, had no power to regulate the procedures by which the legislature may ratify a proposed amendment to the United States Constitution. To do so would inject into the ratification process an element of State regulation not contemplated under article V of the Federal Constitution.

Other factors may be cited to support the conclusion that section 1 of "AN ACT in relation to ratification of proposed amendments to the Constitution of the United States of America" . . . is a nullity.

First, a State law is enduring and cannot be amended or repealed except by the passage of another law following procedures prescribed by the Constitution. Clearly, the 73rd General Assembly has no power to bind subsequent General Assemblies with regard to the procedures by which a proposed amendment to the United States Constitution can be ratified.

Second, a bill enacted by the legislature does not normally become effective until signed by the Governor. Section 1 of "AN ACT in relation to ratification of proposed amendments to the Constitution of the United States of America" . . . was passed by the General Assembly on April 25, 1963, but did not become effective until signed by the Governor on June 25, 1963. Yet, article V of the United States Constitution grants no authority to the Governors or chief executives of the States to participate in the amending process. The General Assembly by attempting to legislate the procedures by which proposed constitutional amendments are to be ratified is, in effect, delegating powers to the Governor; this is an unlawful delegation of power.

Nor can it be said that section 1 of "AN ACT in relation to ratification of proposed amendments to the Constitution of the United States of America" . . . amounts to rules of procedure which are binding on the 78th

General Assembly. Rules of procedure adopted by the 73rd General Assembly are not binding on the 78th General Assembly.

This is not to say that the 78th General Assembly lacks power to make reasonable rules prescribing the kind of majority necessary for ratification, but it must act for itself and solely in its capacity as an instrumentality of the Federal Constitution if it is to do so. As was stated by my predecessor, Attorney General Edward J. Brundage:

> . . . I think it may be strongly argued on the basis of the opinion in the *Hawke case*, that the Constitution commits to the Legislature itself the power to determine for itself, and free from restriction or limitation imposed by *State authority*, what consideration, and the time and manner thereof, it shall give to a proposed amendment to the Federal Constitution, or to a resolution of Congress proposing the same. (emphasis added.) (1919–1920 Op. Atty. Gen. 972, 973–974.)

Article V of the United States Constitution delegates to the "legislature" the power to ratify a proposed amendment to the United States Constitution. Mr. Justice Day in *Hawke* v. *Smith*, 253 U.S. 221, defined a legislature as "the representative body which made the laws of the People."

As to the procedure by which the legislatures are to ratify a proposed amendment, the United States Constitution is silent. Therefore, I am of the opinion that since the legislature has been delegated the power to ratify proposed amendments to the United States Constitution, implicit in this delegation of power is the power to establish reasonable standards and procedures for carrying out the ratification process. The concept that a delegation of express powers carries with it all the implied powers necessary to implement and utilize the express powers is not novel or extraordinary. U.S. Const., art. I, sec. 8; *Goodwine* v. *County of Vermilion*, 271 Ill. 126; *Heidenreich* v. *Ronske*, 26 Ill. 2d 360.

The Illinois General Assembly is the representative body that makes the laws of the People of the State of Illinois. Our General Assembly is bicameral, containing a House of Representatives and a Senate. Accordingly, I am of the opinion that barring the use of extreme standards patently in conflict with article V, each house may, by its own rules, determine how many votes are needed to ratify a proposed amendment to the United States Constitution.

Appendix F

Additional References

Comment. "Rescinding Ratification of Proposed Constitutional Amendments—A Question for the Court." 37 *La. L. Rev.* 896 (1977).

Dodd. "Amending the Federal Constitution." 30 *Yale L. J.* 321 (1921).

Heckman. "Ratification of a Constitutional Amendment: Can a State Change Its Mind?." 6 *Conn. L. Rev.* 28 (1973).

Jameson, John. *A Treatise on Constitutional Conventions*. Callaghan & Co. (Chicago: 1887).

Madison, James. *Notes of the Debates in the Federal Convention of 1787*. W. W. Norton & Co., Inc. (New York: 1969), 104, 560, 609, 649.

Martin. "State Legislative Ratification of Federal Constitutional Amendments: An Overview." 9 *U. of Richmond L. Rev.* 271 (1974–75).

Note. "Proposed Legislation on the Convention Method of Amending the United States Constitution." 85 *Harv. L. Rev. 1612* (1975).

Orfield, Lester. *The Amending of the Federal Constitution*. University of Michigan Press. (Ann Arbor: 1942).

Planell, Raymond. "The Equal Rights Amendment: Will States Be Allowed to Change Their Minds?" 49 *Notre Dame Lawyer* 657 (1974).

"Symposium: Article Five of the Constitution." 66 *Mich. L. Rev.* 837, 884 (1968).

Index to Text

Samuel S. Freedman, judge of the Connecticut Superior Court, is a visiting lecturer in law at Yale Law School, and a former state legislator and legislative commissioner for the State of Connecticut. Pamela J. Naughton has been a member of the senatorial staff of Vice-president Walter F. Mondale and a law clerk in the office of the U.S. attorney in Minneapolis, Minnesota. She is currently a student at Yale Law School.

The manuscript was edited by Sherwyn T. Carr. The book was designed by Richard Kinney. The typeface for the text is Times Roman, designed under the supervision of Stanley Morison about 1932, and the display face is Souvenir.

The paperback edition is bound in Carolina Cover CIS, and the hardcover edition is bound in Joanna Mills' Linson 2 over binder's boards. Manufactured in the United States of America.